Focus ON THE Wild

SAVING SOUTH TEXAS WILDLIFE

The Valley Land Fund Wildlife Photo Contest IV

Front Cover: Crested Caracara
   Photographer: John Cancalosi / Landowner: Matt and Patty Gorges
Back Cover: American Alligator
   Photographer: Derrick Hamrick and Roberta E. Summers / Landowner: Jim and Kathy Collins and Carolyn Cook Landrum – Cook Ranch Properties

First Printing, 2001
   Text and Photography Copyright © 2001 Valley Land Fund, Inc.

ISBN 0-9710604-0-1

Published by Valley Land Fund, Inc.

The Valley Land Fund
   2400 North 10th Street, Suite A
   McAllen, Texas 78501

Website: www.valleylandfund.com

Land Trust Office
   Phone (956) 971-8550 / Fax (956) 971-8565
   Email: valleylf@aol.com

Wildlife Photo Contest Office
   Phone (956) 686-6429 / Fax (956) 686-1909
   Email: contest@valleylandfund.com

Managing Editor: Ron Smith
Copy Editor: Jan Seale
Printing coordination and color work: Bob Carter, Carter and Associates, Boulder, Colorado
Book and cover design: Don Breeden and Robert J. Scott, Breeden/McCumber/Gonzalez, Inc., Brownsville, Texas
Printing: Gateway Printing, Edinburg, Texas

Printed in the U.S.A.

Dedicated to
A. CLAYTON SCRIBNER
and to the memory of
LYNETTE L. SCRIBNER (1907-1992)

For nearly 60 years they loved the land and each other. Together they dedicated time, energy and money to those organizations charged with conserving our natural flora and fauna. They came to the Valley in 1980 and helped many of our local organizations, but none so much as The Valley Land Fund. As founding members and stalwart supporters, they helped us learn, grow and prosper. Lynette is gone now, but Clayton, at age 94, continues to encourage and inspire.

Ralph Paonessa/Joe Michael Castellano

CONTENTS

David Welling/Pérez Ranch

PREFACE

Man can have but one interest in nature, namely, to see himself reflected or interpreted there, and we quickly neglect both poet and philosopher who fail to satisfy, in some measure, this feeling.

— *John Burroughs*

No humans had ever seen her. She had seen them from her secret places as they walked the trails of the refuge. Now in the shadows, she lay flat on a mesquite limb curving downward to run a few feet above the ground, her brownish-gray fur blending almost perfectly with the bark.

A few feet away, dawnlight stippled the trail. All senses were alert as she waited. The short ears cupped forward. The long tail whipped once. A scent on the downwind had stirred her hunger: a noisy, milling flock of long-tailed birds approached.

The small cat slipped off the branch, and supple muscles suddenly became steel. A wavelet of warning sound had slapped her ears and stopped her like a shot for half a heartbeat! Then there was nothing where she had been but gray branches, green leaves and shafts of sunlight. What remained was a Memory and a Hope.

In a few months, a photograph of this Jaguarundi, smallest and rarest of the South

Texas wild cats, would be featured in a magazine or a book. Photographers and naturalists would agree that Hope had been answered. "What luck!" they would mutter. "What a shot!" It would be the first authenticated record in many years of this species in South Texas.

You will not see such a photograph in our book...not yet...but someday you might, perhaps due in part to The Valley Land Fund, a group of citizens dedicated to many projects, such as preserving the green corridors along the Rio Grande, the brushlands of the ranch country and the wetlands and woodlots of South Padre Island. However, you will not be disappointed in the gallery displayed here, the result of our Wildlife Photo Contest. It is not merely a picture book for a coffee table but rather a melding of scientific knowledge, personal experience and the art of the photographer.

While reading the previous contest's book, a friend pretended to leave the harried adult world, approaching the text and pictures as a child would, with open innocence, full of the serenity of that stage of life when time seems to stretch forever before you. Relate this to the above quotation by the great naturalist John Burroughs, and you may find yourself reflected in these photographs, not as a separate entity,

but as a being connected to the beauty and diversity of the natural world. We do, indeed, become "a part of all that we have met."

Stephen Jay Gould, the eminent Harvard professor and scientist, recently lamented that we are experiencing nature more and more vicariously, a virtual reality syndrome, one might say. And so, after you have enjoyed these pictures, seek what they represent. You will find yourself in realms you may have only imagined—not of the sterile streets of towns, nor the rude race of freeways.

These places exist in side trips off farm roads, along the winding paths of refuges and the trails of ranchlands . . .so close, yet apart from your daily scramble. This will not be virtual reality, nor mere scenery through tinted car windows, nor part of the world of commodities in malls. On the contrary, you will become aware that these realms are bejeweled with life: topaz butterflies, emerald birds and ruby beetles, all enveloped in heady scents and musical sounds.

This book can be your portal.

Enter and focus on the Wild.

Ron Smith
Pharr, Texas, and Hubbard Lake, Michigan

THE LEGACY OF CONSERVATION

When I think of how I have come to be involved in The Valley Land Fund, I have to smile at a story of an early Valley wildlife encounter by my father Charles. Dad moved to the Valley in the late thirties from the Midwest and soon was invited by Alfred King to hunt in King Ranch brush country.

Tom Urban/King Ranch

As Dad sat in a blind, a huge blacksnake attempted to join him. He didn't know how valuable the blacksnake was to ranchers and began blasting away with his deer rifle, finally killing the innocent critter.

The ranch hands scurried to Dad, wondering what the heck he was shooting at. When they discovered their friendly blacksnake, affectionately named Luke, lying there lifeless, they weren't too happy with this tinhorn. They drove Dad back to the ranch house and suggested that the next outdoor adventure he went on should be with a fishing pole in his hands!

The Valley Land Fund has great appeal to me. I'm proud to be given an opportunity to work with others who know the importance of preserving nature, who work for a legacy in which our children can continue to enjoy the animal and plant species unique to the Valley. Our group's goals of conservation and stewardship offer our best hope to salvage as much as possible in The Magic Valley and adjacent lands.

When the Great Horned Owl flies across the face of the moon, little is heard but the beating of our hearts. The magnificent web of life calls us to enjoy, preserve, and share it.

Together, we can make a difference. But we must not linger.

> *Kirk Clark*
> *McAllen, Texas*

Kirk Clark, businessman and VLF board member, has a deep concern for the ecology of South Texas. He is also a poet whose work reflects his love of nature.

6

GRAND PRIZE TEAMS

Rosemary and Cleve Breedlove hosted the Grand Prize teams for a breakfast at The Inn at Chachalaca Bend near Los Fresnos. The Breedloves have developed 40 acres surrounding their unique bed and breakfast inn as a visitation area for birders, butterfly enthusiasts and botanists. The photo was taken in their backyard, which is situated on a bend in Resaca de las Antonias, an oxbow fed by Resaca de las Cuates.

(Front row, standing) Nicole Woodhouse, Karen Fitzgerald (Front row, seated) Larry Ditto, Audrey Martin, Greg Lasley, Marlee Payne, Bud Payne (Second row) Roberto Yzaguirre, Fran Yzaguirre, Sean Fitzgerald, Suzanne Shepard, John Martin, Colleen Hook, Derrick Hamrick, Roberta E. Summers (Third row) Dr. Steve Shepard, Glenn Hayes, Bill Draker, Dr. Gary M. Schwarz. *Photo by Ruth Hoyt*

WILDLIFE PHOTO CONTEST IV

The Lower Rio Grande Valley teems with wildlife, providing a unique blend of flora and fauna that occurs nowhere else in North America. Species from the Desert Southwest meet others from the southeastern states, and those from the North join many that are more typical of Mexico and Central America. All are drawn to the hospitable climate and to tracts of thorn-scrub woodland and the sprawling ranches that dot the southern tip of Texas.

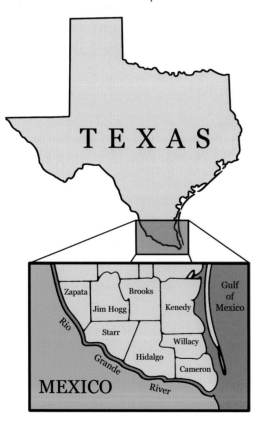

It is here that the Ocelot and Jaguarundi still prowl the thickets, albeit in diminished numbers, and birds like the Green Jay, Plain Chachalaca, Altamira Oriole, and Ringed Kingfisher thrill birders from around the world. Tropical butterflies flash their rainbow hues amid equally colorful wildflowers by day, while the night showcases the shrill songs of rare frogs and toads that range no farther north. Even the names of the trees and shrubs that harbor these exotic wildlife forms—ébano, tepeguaje, retama, granjeno, colima—reflect a subtropical treasure-trove unparalleled in the United States.

This wildlife paradise is by no means secure, however. Clearing of the native woodlands for agriculture and for residential and commercial development has taken a heavy toll. No more than 2% of the land in Texas is in public hands, and the preservation of this vital habitat thus depends on private landowners. It was to help preserve these treasures for future generations that The Valley Land Fund was formed in 1987, and in 1994, this local non-profit group staged its first Wildlife Photo Contest.

Held every other year, the contest pairs photographers from across the country with private landowners, and both share equally in prize money that has grown from an initial $77,250 in 1994 to $130,000 in 2000, making it the richest photo contest in the world.

In 2000, amateur and professional photographers, numbering 150, worked from January 1 through June 30, either alone or in teams of two, on their selected tracts of land. They shot countless rolls of film and were allowed three entries for each of 50 different classes in five broad divisions: Birds, Mammals, Insects and Arachnids, Reptiles and Amphibians, and Special Categories. It was a contest where the image of a butterfly or beetle was worth as much as that of a Bobcat or White-tailed buck. No subject was too small, for none is unimportant in the web of life. The stunning results of this photographic treasure hunt are showcased in this book.

In establishing its photo contest, the VLF had three stated goals: to heighten public awareness of the wildlife diversity in the Rio Grande Valley, to create an incentive for landowners to protect wildlife habitat, and to obtain incomparable images for educational purposes. The teams of photographers and landowners had a common goal and shared equally in the labor and rewards. The real winner, however, was the wildlife depicted here, for the contest will help preserve the vital habitat so desperately needed.

John and Gloria Tveten
Baytown, Texas

Authors and photographers John and Gloria Tveten are preeminent experts on all Texas flora and fauna. They wrote a nature column for The Houston Chronicle *for 24 years and have published many books celebrating Texas wildlife.*

VLF WILDLIFE PHOTOGRAPHERS OF THE YEAR
First Grand Prize-winning Photographers: Larry Ditto and Greg Lasley

Larry Ditto and Greg Lasley/Bud and Jimmy Payne

The looks on the faces of Bud and Marlee Payne on the night we previewed some of our early photos from their Kenedy County ranch were one of our highlights for the 2000 VLF contest. "We had no idea all those beautiful animals lived on our ranch!" was Marlee's ecstatic response. Every landowner who participated will probably smile as they read this and think, "We had the same reaction." That's what it's all about—pride in having the opportunity to play a part in the conservation of this very special little corner of God's creation.

The entire contest was like that for us. In spite of the clouds, wind and rainouts, almost every day revealed something new and wonderful about those isolated 7,400 acres of coastal prairie. Maybe the best day for Larry came on a March afternoon at a small pond in the west pasture of the ranch. He had seen a night heron or two there and thought he might manage a few photos late in the day. About an hour before sunset, all sorts of wading birds began arriving and during the last few minutes of "shooting" light, hundreds of Great Egrets, Cattle Egrets, Great Blue Herons and White Ibis appeared. There were so many, so close, he couldn't decide which ones to photograph.

For Greg, one of many highlights was discovering a sizable population of Botteri's Sparrows scattered throughout the ranch's grasslands. The species occurs nowhere else in Texas except in the southernmost counties, and rarely at that.

At first glance, we might seem like an odd couple. Larry was employed by the U.S. Fish and Wildlife Service for 30 years while Greg was an

Austin police officer for 25 years. Each of us, however, has been involved with birds and wildlife for many years and each has been photographing nature subjects since the 1970's. Greg retired from law enforcement in 1997 and started leading birding trips for Victor Emanuel Nature Tours. Larry retired in 1999 to focus on photography.

If there is a confession to make, it is that both of us are partial to birds and bird photography. But, preferences had to be put aside for the contest, which pushed us into many unaccustomed pursuits—such as photographing spiders in cactus, watching the evening sky for bats, and doing the low-crawl to close the distance on a feeding jackrabbit. This was truly "Iron Man" photography. We got in shape, got a tan, picked up a few ticks, lost a little weight, lost a lot of sleep... all for that great shot no one else would get. But it was fun!

We sincerely appreciate the efforts of our mutual good friend, Steve Bentsen, who knew both of us were looking for a contest partner and helped get us together.

He must have anticipated we would offer some competition to his own chances to win the contest but thought first of our friendship. And to John Martin we say "Thanks" for introducing us to Bud and Jimmy Payne. This was their first go at the contest as landowners, and they

probably had some serious apprehension about letting two strangers roam around on their property for six months. Bud and Jimmy placed a lot of trust in us, but now friendship has replaced doubts.

Most importantly, we owe a tremendous debt of gratitude to our wives, Glenda and Cheryl, who patiently accepted our prolonged absences and cheerfully welcomed us home for brief "vacations" from our photographic "work." Throughout the contest, they urged us to buy all the film and equipment we wanted and to take all the time we needed to win this thing. Well, not really, but they were supportive. One of the many happy footnotes to the story was the arrival of Larry and Glenda's first grandchild, born during the contest.

What a wonderful event this contest has become! Thank you, Valley Land Fund and contest sponsors, for making it a reality. Your partnership has produced incredible success in the promotion of habitat and wildlife conservation in South Texas. By attracting photographers from across the country, the contest has achieved recognition throughout the photographic and conservation world. We are especially proud to be the first Texans to finish as your First Grand Prize winners.

Gracias, amigos y que les vaya bien.

> *Larry Ditto and Greg Lasley*
> *McAllen, Texas, and Austin, Texas*

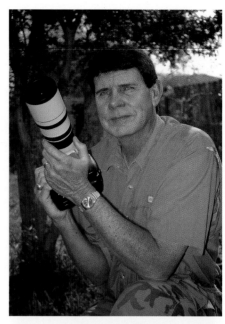

Larry Ditto,
McAllen, Texas
*Photo by
Susan Ditto*

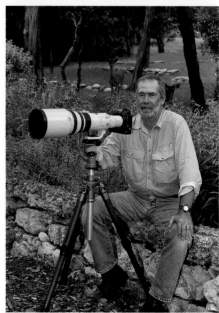

Greg Lasley,
Austin, Texas
*Photo by
John Ingram*

VLF LANDOWNERS OF THE YEAR
First Grand Prize-winning Landowners: Bud and Jimmy Payne

Being born and raised in South Texas, we thought we knew quite a bit about its critters and surrounds. That is, until shutterbugs crawled onto our Kenedy County ranch in the form of Larry Ditto and Greg Lasley in January 2000 for the photo contest. And what a memorable and educational experience that was and continues to be!

Our ranch is located in the King Ranch Corridor between Highways 77 and 281, originally part of the Ball Ranch. It consists of three topographical characteristics: savannah grasslands with mesquite mottes; cayos y lomas (hills interspersed with shallow, salt-oriented lakes); and low-lying sacahuistal grass flats. For a South Texas ranch, it has a tremendous amount of natural water, often seasonally. Only 20 miles from the coast, we get more rain than ranches farther west, but we are also prone to flooding. Abundant water certainly adds to the area's uniqueness—so much so that after Larry's first couple of times getting stuck, he felt compelled to purchase a four-wheel drive pickup.

Although we probably had the typical landowner skepticism at first, it did not take us long to realize what a treasure to the natural world Larry and Greg are. They both treated us, and especially our ranch, with utmost consideration and respect. It was great to see tall Larry (6' 8 ") in a floating tube in pursuit of the ever-elusive grebe nest shot, or Greg seining a

pond to establish the presence of a Tiger Salamander. (We never even knew we had salamanders of any kind.)

We know so much more about our land and resources now, and we are blessed to be able to share with others, through our team's photos and knowledge, the natural world of our ranch. And thanks to Larry and Greg for winning—they really deserved it. An additional outcome of this landowner-photographer relationship has been a bond of friendship which will last a lifetime.

Our family has been farming and ranching in South Texas for over 40 years. We would like to thank our father E.J. Payne for teaching us to be stewards of the land. His basic tenet was to slow down and really look at the land, always leaving it better than when he started. We feel obliged to be such stewards. We and our cow partner Peter McBride use cell (paddocks) grazing that allows our land to rest much of the time, thereby enhancing our native grasses and habitat. We use suspension fencing around our cells to allow free-flow of wildlife throughout the ranch. We believe in conservation and protection of our native ecosystem. We fear for the lack of care and possible disappearance of the native habitat of South Texas.

We would especially like to thank The Valley Land Fund, its staff and sponsors, as well as all the untiring

photographers. And a special thanks to our ranch foreman and strawboss, Bud's wife Marlee, who loves and appreciates the ranch as much as we do. And most of all, thanks to God for His grace in allowing us the use of this land as His stewards.

Bud and Jimmy Payne
Weslaco, Texas

Businessmen Bud and Jimmy Payne are very active in The Valley Land Fund. They are dedicated to preserving the area's natural treasures.

Jimmy Payne and Marlee and Bud Payne, Weslaco, Texas
Photo by Ruth Hoyt

SECOND GRAND PRIZE WINNERS

It was amazing how accustomed and gentle a lot of the animals became to me. I set up in a clearing to photograph a large buck. He came out behind me and was well aware that I was there. I started talking to him and he did not leave. He walked past me and went to the corn that I had put out.

I am a serious amateur, not trying to be a professional, but I do try to sell a few slides, mostly to pay expenses. I like photographing all wildlife but put most of my emphasis on photographing birds.

Many wildlife photographers photograph in places such as parks where animals have become accustomed to people and are easier to approach. Photographing animals that are truly wild is much more of a challenge. Also, the time frame, the heat and wind were unique to this contest and South Texas. (B.D.)

Photographers:
Bill Draker and Glenn Hayes

The environment does not care about the human motive or political lean of those who are responsible for its protection, only that it be protected. With the rapid growth in population and development, the environment needs all of us doing our part, and the sooner we learn to work together, the better off our lands will be. The Valley Land Fund is leading the way in showcasing these kinds of diverse partnerships, coming together and proving that we can indeed not only get along but thrive together. (G.S.)

Landowners:
Dr. Gary M. Schwarz, Dr. Steve Shepard and Partners – Tecomate Ranch

Bill Draker and Glenn Hayes/Dr. Gary M. Schwarz, Dr. Steve Shepard and Partners – Tecomate Ranch

THIRD GRAND PRIZE WINNERS

Sean Fitzgerald and Jeremy Woodhouse/Roberto and Fran Yzaguirre

Late one evening, our ranch hand brought us a bucket with a burlap bag tied over the top. He told us it was a red and black snake, and from what we could see it appeared to be a milk snake. We figured we would photograph and release it the next morning. The next morning, however, it was gone. We finally found it, under one of our beds. It wasn't a milk snake—it was a Texas Coral Snake.

South Texas is an absolute treasure of biological diversity. Unfortunately, the habitat and weather that breed that diversity can be brutal on a photographer's mind and body. And unlike in most parks, the wildlife is not accustomed to humans. It all adds up to an extreme but intensely rewarding photographic challenge. (S.F.)

Photographers:
Sean Fitzgerald and Jeremy Woodhouse

Our land is typical South Texas brush country. It has been left in its natural state and is unique only in that it is a tract of land that is fairly isolated and has been subjected to a minimum amount of "improvement." Prevalent wildlife includes deer, javelinas, turkeys and other birds—all native to South Texas.

Our ancestors understood that this Valley was a rich and bountiful place. Unfortunately, they also believed that it was inexhaustible. We forgive them for what they may have destroyed in their ignorance. However, today it is essential that we understand what we have inherited, and that we be responsible for protecting it so that it can be passed along to future generations.

Landowners:
Roberto and Fran Yzaguirre

FOURTH GRAND PRIZE WINNERS

I had memorable experiences with numerous species, including a six-foot Western Diamondback Rattlesnake photographed from two feet, a 14-foot American Alligator who would have loved to eat me, and the Greater Roadrunner that appeared out of nowhere only to eat mealworms out of our hands.

My work has and always will be passionate. My mission is to show the world what is left and to utilize every skill to make the image come to life and, therefore, encourage people to understand that all creatures great or small are worth preserving.

South Texas is unique in its diversity of life in prolific quantities, especially birds. Also unique is its desert-like habitat supporting an array of reptilian life, along with numerous mammal species from the little Mexican Ground Squirrel to the White-tailed Deer. The insect life, especially at night, is awe-inspiring. (D.H.)

Photographers:
Derrick Hamrick and Roberta E. Summers

Derrick Hamrick and Roberta E. Summers/Jim and Kathy Collins and Carolyn Cook Landrum – Cook Ranch Properties

Our land is special because the ranches are large enough to support a vast number of habitat combinations. The bird life is most prevalent, because the ranches provide areas that vary from desert-like brushland to large and lush ponds.

Landowners:
Jim and Kathy Collins and Carolyn Cook Landrum – Cook Ranch Properties

FIFTH GRAND PRIZE WINNERS

Tom Urban/King Ranch

The wildlife I find most interesting and challenging is raptors. Very rewarding as well as educational to photograph are nests with young. Most raptors I've worked exhibit different types of behavior and prey selection. These birds are masters of flight, integrating strength, power and beauty.

I have photographed in four other countries and have visited some spectacular national parks and refuges in the United States. But none of these lands can compete with the biodiversity of plants and wildlife found in South Texas.

Photographer:
Tom Urban

Thought for future generations about the natural environment of the Valley: Preserve native grasses and trees and destroy no more wildlife habitat.

Landowners:
King Ranch

The greatness of a nation and its moral progress can be judged by the way its animals are treated.
— Gandhi

THE WINNING PHOTOGRAPHS

Winning photographs are presented according to the categories of the Wildlife Photo Contest. However, not all species in the category titles were photographed or won prizes.

Larry Ditto and Greg Lasley/Bud and Jimmy Payne

Tom Urban/King Ranch

David Welling/Pérez Ranch

Bill Draker and Glenn Hayes/
Dr. Gary M. Schwarz, Dr. Steve Shepard and Partners

Bill Burns/Burns Ranch

David Welling/Pérez Ranch

David Welling/Pérez Ranch

Sean Fitzgerald and Jeremy Woodhouse/
Roberto and Fran Yzagurirre

BIRDS

A route of evanescence
With a revolving wheel;
A resonance of emerald,
A rush of cochineal...

— Emily Dickinson

Bill Draker and Glenn Hayes/
Dr. Gary M. Schwarz, Dr. Steve Shepard and Partners

Adjectives extraordinaire have been used to describe the power and beauty of birds, the marvel of flight and migration, their adaptability and planet-encompassing presence. We are awed by what these creatures are capable of accomplishing, by both the simplicity and complexity of their lives. We shake our heads at the fact that mere grams of feather, muscle and bone can travel inordinate distances with nothing other than a relatively thin layer of fat for fuel, bringing them at the end of their journey to the same patch of forest where they came into being.

Species variation allows for almost every possible habitat niche to be populated, whether it be the frigid Arctic, the tropical rain forests of the Amazon basin, or the far reaches of the earth's oceans. Avian life, over the millennia, has adapted to various types of weather, food, altitude and environment. So, even if we are just delving into their intriguing existence, we are already completely captivated by what we perceive regarding their innate strength and power.

I can recall, as a child, first becoming aware of the birds that surrounded me, and how, as the years passed, friends and acquaintances further opened my eyes to this specialness. I was astounded by flight and mesmerized by both vivid colors and cryptic patterning. But, it was only in my later years that I was bitten by the so-called "Birding Bug." Suffice it to say, once the drive to "bird" took hold, I was locked in for life.

It is easy to recognize the appeal and fascination of birds, but every now and again, we are stung by the realization that their very presence can be thoroughly enchanting. As I stood one day on the parapet of Fort Jefferson overlooking the clear waters off the Dry Tortugas, I glimpsed an almost translucent form emerging from the hazy air. Spellbound, I watched as the easy languid flight of a White-tailed Tropicbird brought this exquisite flier's pale elegance right before my eyes.

A number of times it circled the small bay that separated Bush and Garden Keys, and occasionally, it ventured so close to my lookout that I was tempted to reach out and try to touch it. In time, as with all things that defy possession, it drifted away, fading into the distance, leaving me with an almost physical sense of loss. How I wanted that incredibly beautiful vision to return, to continue to address me, to startle me!

I chuckle when I realize how little I truly know and understand about the avian resource that shares my world, but I am also cognizant of the fact that my passion for that knowledge and understanding has brought me to a wiser approach to life. The recognition of my role as steward has led to practical consequences where my responsibility is crucial and critical.

The more we open our eyes to discovery, the fuller life can be embraced. Be it bird, butterfly, plant or mammal—observe, appreciate and defend. But especially, enjoy our birds!

Father Thomas Pincelli
Harlingen, Texas

Parish priest Father Tom Pincelli is a premier birder, columnist and tour guide. He is the force behind the famous Rio Grande Valley Birding Festival and serves on the boards of numerous nature organizations.

BIRDS OF PREY

Crested Caracara
Crested Caracaras often feed on carrion, so when we found a dead cow in a pasture, we set up a blind to see what would happen. Finally, two beautiful caracaras began to feed and, when perched on the carcass with crops bulging, they created a true South Texas scene.
First Place
Photographer: Larry Ditto and Greg Lasley
Landowner: Bud and Jimmy Payne

Canon EOS 1N with Canon EF 600mm f/4 L lens;
f/5.6 @ 1/250 sec.; Fuji Provia 100F pushed one stop

Turkey Vulture (wings spread); Black Vulture

As I watched the vultures on the carcass, the temperature dropped a few degrees. The Turkey Vulture must have also felt it and suddenly spread its wings to get some of the late afternoon sun.

Second Place
Photographer: J. Stephen Lay
Landowner: Minten Ranch

Nikon F100 with Nikon 600mm f/4 lens; f/5.6 or f/8 @ 1/125 sec.; Kodachrome 200

White-tailed Hawk

An adult White-tailed Hawk would sometimes land on the limb before it flew into the nest to feed its two young. The frustrating part was watching the parents bring in two-foot or three-foot long snakes and my missing all shots due to manual focus.

Third Place
Photographer: Derrick Hamrick and Roberta E. Summers
Landowner: Jim and Kathy Collins and Carolyn Cook Landrum – Cook Ranch Properties

Canon EOS 3 with Canon 400 f/2.8 IS lens and 1.4x teleconverter; f/6.3 @ 1/250 sec.; Fuji Sensia 100

WADING BIRDS

‹ Great Blue Heron
Our resident heron would alternate between two water holes, so it was good fortune to have him fly in during one morning session in my blind. He would come in to feast on the plentiful supply of Rio Grande Leopard Frogs.

First Place
Photographer: Sean Fitzgerald and Jeremy Woodhouse
Landowner: Roberto and Fran Yzaguirre

Canon EOS 3 with EF 600 f/4 lens;
f/5.6 @ 1/250 sec.; Kodak E100VS

Cattle Egret
A male Cattle Egret in peak breeding plumage was sunning and preening itself on the edge of the water hole. The soft evening crosslighting, which I prefer to flat frontal lighting, really drew me to take the shot.

Second Place
Photographer: Sean Fitzgerald and Jeremy Woodhouse
Landowner: Roberto and Fran Yzaguirre

Canon EOS 3 with EF 600 f/4 lens;
f/4 @ 1/250 sec.; Kodak E100VS

Least Bittern
I was in a float tube trying to get close to some cattails where I had seen a Least Bittern the day before. Motion caught my eye, and one climbed out onto the cattails and peered at me in curiosity.

Third Place
Photographer: Larry Ditto and Greg Lasley
Landowner: Bud and Jimmy Payne

Canon EOS 1N with Canon EF 300mm f/2.8 lens and 2x teleconverter;
f/5.6 @ 1/250 sec.; Fuji Velvia pushed one stop

RAILS, GALLINULES and COOTS

< Least Grebe

The Least Grebe took about 30 minutes to adjust to my presence. Once everything settled down, she climbed onto the floating nest and began incubating her eggs. Eventually, while preening, the bird pulled a breast feather that stuck to the tip of her bill. What a wonderful reward for my hours of sitting in chest-deep water waiting for something unusual to occur!

First Place
(Fourth Place: Birds Division)
Photographer: Larry Ditto and Greg Lasley
Landowner: Bud and Jimmy Payne

Canon EOS 1N with Canon 300mm AF f/2.8 lens and 2x teleconverter; f/5.6 @ 1/125 sec.; Fuji Velvia pushed one stop

Virginia Rail *(Top Right)*

A Virginia Rail came out to forage within feet of my blind late one January evening with the last rays of sun showing the bird's plumage beautifully.

Second Place
Photographer: Larry Ditto and Greg Lasley
Landowner: Bud and Jimmy Payne

Canon EOS 3 with Canon EF 600mm f/4 lens; f/4 @ 1/125 sec.; Fuji Velvia pushed one stop

American Coot

American Coots are far from being the prettiest birds around, but all that changes when one can photograph them in a pond of blooming water lilies. This bird seemed to be yawning as I slowly approached in my floating blind.

Third Place
Photographer: Larry Ditto and Greg Lasley
Landowner: Bud and Jimmy Payne

Canon EOS 1N with Canon 300mm AF f/2.8 lens and 2x teleconverter; f/5.6 @ 1/125 sec.; Fuji Velvia pushed one stop

WATERFOWL

Mallard

I had been set up at this water pond before dawn. Just as light broke, a flight of ducks splashed down. As sunlight painted the pond, a duck started preening herself. The mosquitoes I'd been enduring were worth this moment.

First Place
Photographer: Tom Urban
Landowner: King Ranch

Canon F1 with Canon 400mm 2.8L lens and 1.4x-A teleconverter; f/4 @ 1/125 sec.; Kodak E100VS

Northern Shoveler

From my water level blind I had been looking for a unique behavioral type of shot, and I knew that I had it when I panned my 800mm lens inches above the water and fired upon the Northern Shoveler as it tipped to feed.

Third Place

Photographer: Derrick Hamrick and Roberta E. Summers
Landowner: Jim and Kathy Collins and Carolyn Cook Landrum – Cook Ranch Properties

Canon EOS 1N-RS with 400 mm f/2.8 IS lens and 2x teleconverter; f/6.3 @ 1/500 sec.; Fuji Sensia

Black-bellied Whistling-Duck

Red-eared Turtles and many water birds, including Roseate Spoonbills, foraged by this grassy bar when the water level was right. Black-bellied Whistling-Ducks were among the wariest and seldom came this close to the blind.

Second Place

Photographer: Cliff Beittel
Landowner: Frank D. Yturria – Yturria Ranch

Canon EOS 3 with Canon 600mm f/4L lens; f/8 @ 1/200 sec.; Fuji Velvia pushed one stop

SHOREBIRDS

‹ **Greater Yellowlegs**
My partner and I captured many excellent photographs on this shallow wetland during the two months it was flooded. Two days before the pond was dry and while many frogs, minnows and tadpoles were concentrated in it, I placed a blind nearby to capture the feeding activity of predatory birds. Just after sunrise on the second day, a Greater Yellowlegs arrived and promptly caught a fully developed tadpole...right in front of my lens.

First Place
(Fifth Place: Birds Division)
Photographer: Larry Ditto and Greg Lasley
Landowner: Bud and Jimmy Payne

Canon EOS 3 with Canon 600mm AF f/4 lens and 1.4x teleconverter; f/6.3 @ 1/250 sec.; Fuji Velvia pushed one stop

Black-necked Stilt
A Black-necked Stilt was feeding shortly after sunrise. These birds have longer legs in proportion to their bodies than any other species.

Second Place
Photographer: Mike Kelly
Landowner: J.A. Jr. and Sue Ann Garcia – Garcia Ranch

Nikon F5 with Nikon AF-S ED 600mm f/4 D IF lens and TC-14F teleconverter; f/5.6 @ 1/125 sec.; Fuji Velvia pushed one stop

Greater Yellowlegs
A migrant Greater Yellowlegs stopped to rest on a small pond. I took a number of shots as it foraged along the edge of the water, but when it stopped to stretch, I was only able to get one shot.

Third Place
Photographer: Larry Ditto and Greg Lasley
Landowner: Bud and Jimmy Payne

Canon EOS 3 with Canon EF 600mm f/4 lens and 1.4x teleconverter; f/5.6 @ 1/250 sec.; Fuji Velvia pushed one stop

HUMMINGBIRDS

‹ **Buff-bellied Hummingbird**
To freeze the rapid wing beats of this tiny bird, I used flash on both the bird and the background. After two days of setting up light stands and flashes, I sat for six hours near a feeder and only managed to get a few shots.
First Place
Photographer: Ralph Paonessa
Landowner: Joe Michael Castellano – Castellano Ranch

Canon EOS 3 with Canon EF 70-200mm f/2.8L lens and EF 1.4x teleconverter; f/22 @ 1/200 sec. with multiple flash @ 1/20,000 sec.; Fuji Velvia

Buff-bellied Hummingbird
Buff-bellied Hummingbirds are common here in the Valley and a prime example of our sub-tropical fauna. This image, which captures the bird's skill of hanging motionless in the air, was one of many taken over several days as the hummer came in briefly to feed on Red Yucca flowers.
Third Place
Photographer: Lynn Bieber-Weir and Ray Bieber
Landowner: Patric and Amy Ginsbach, Wayne and Chris Westphal – Palm Gardens, Inc.

Canon EOS 3 with Canon EF 500 f/4 lens, 1.4x teleconverter and 12.5mm extension tube; f/8 @ 1/30 sec.; Kodak E100VS

Buff-bellied Hummingbird
It took us several days to find this nest saddled on a branch of an ebony tree and perfectly camouflaged with lichens. It contained a single well-feathered young hummingbird, and we photographed it from high atop a very tall stepladder.
Second Place
Photographer: John and Gloria Tveten
Landowner: Rosemary and Cleve Breedlove – The Inn at Chachalaca Bend

MInolta X-700 with 100mm macro lens and Sunpack ringlight; f/11 @ 1/60 sec.; Fuji Velvia

BLACKBIRDS, ORIOLES and TANAGERS

Great-tailed Grackle
A female grackle had just emerged from a nest site in cattails along the edge of a pond. The late evening light gave her a splendid appearance as she prepared to go out in search of food for her young.
First Place
Photographer: Larry Ditto and Greg Lasley
Landowner: Bud and Jimmy Payne

Canon EOS 1N with Canon EF f/2.8 lens and 2x teleconverter; f/5.6 @ 1/250 sec.; Fuji Velvia pushed one stop

Great-tailed Grackle

One morning while photographing waterfowl, I noticed that an occasional grackle would sometimes bathe along the shallows of a particular sandbar and defend its bathing area by driving away waterfowl several times its size.

Second Place

Photographer: Derrick Hamrick and Roberta E. Summers
Landowner: Jim and Kathy Collins and Carolyn Cook Landrum – Cook Ranch Properties

Canon EOS 3 with Canon 400mm f/2.8 IS lens and 2x teleconverter; f/5.6 @ 1/250 sec.; Fuji Sensia 100

Western Meadowlark

I set up a few feeders around some blooming brush and hoped that the birds would come. Many did, but I had very few days with good light. When the sun did shine, I had to get busy.

Third Place

Photographer: Bill Draker and Glenn Hayes
Landowner: Dr. Gary M. Schwarz, Dr. Steve Shepard and Partners – Tecomate Ranch

Canon EOS 3 with Canon 500mm f/4 IS lens and 1.4x teleconverter; f/14 @ 1/125 sec.; Fuji Sensia 100

FLYCATCHERS and KINGBIRDS

‹ Scissor-tailed Flycatcher

The flycatcher, building its nest about 15 feet up, tolerated my approach as long as I moved slowly. By using a telephoto at minimum aperture and a fast shutter speed, I was able to stop the motion and blur the background.

First Place
(Second Place: Birds Division)
Photographer: Derrick Hamrick and Roberta E. Summers
Landowner: Jim and Kathy Collins and Carolyn Cook Landrum – Cook Ranch Properties

Canon EOS 1N-RS with Canon 400mm f/2.8 IS lens; f/2.8 @ 1/2000 sec.; Fuji Sensia 100

Vermilion Flycatcher

The male and female both work in the Vermilion family, making this an exciting and active nest to watch. They keep it clean by collecting the small fecal sacs, which look like white trash bags.

Second Place
Photographer: Marilyn Moseley La Mantia and Brenda Moseley Holt
Landowner: Jack Scoggins, Jr. – Starr Feedyards, Inc.

Canon EOS 1N with Canon 400mm f/2.8 lens, EF 12 extension tube and 430 EZ flash; f/8 @ 1/90 sec.; Fuji Provia III

Couch's Kingbird

I like to sit in a spot that would give me more than just one subject to photograph. This kingbird came to the blind I had set up near a water hole. Many different critters will come to water when it is hot and dry.

Third Place
Photographer: Bill Draker and Glenn Hayes
Landowner: Dr. Gary M. Schwarz, Dr. Steve Shepard and Partners – Tecomate Ranch

Canon EOS 3 with Canon 500mm f/4 IS lens and 2x teleconverter; f/14 @ 1/125 sec.; Fuji Sensia 100

KINGFISHERS

Green Kingfisher
Kingfishers are sometimes easy to photograph when they pause
before diving for fish. That was the case for this female
Green Kingfisher.
First Place
Photographer: Bill Burns
Landowner: Bill Burns – Burns Ranch

*Canon EOS 3 with Canon 100-400 IS lens;
f/5.6 @ 1/500; Kodak E100VS*

Belted Kingfisher
This kingfisher appeared for only one day in February to fish on the pond, and I was lucky to capture some images of its hovering flights and dives for fish.

Third Place
Photographer: Mike Kelly
Landowner: J.A. Jr. and Sue Ann Garcia – Garcia Ranch

Nikon F5 with Nikon AF-S ED 500mm f/4 D IF lens and TC-20E teleconverter; f/8 @ 1/250 sec.; Fuji Velvia pushed one stop

Belted Kingfisher
Kingfishers surprise their prey (usually fish) by diving from a hovering position or perch into the water; their accuracy is amazing. I saw this bird catch dragonfly nymphs and minnows. Occasionally, she even got a bill full of pondweed which was discarded in favor of an all-meat diet.

Second Place
Photographer: Larry Ditto and Greg Lasley
Landowner: Bud and Jimmy Payne

Canon EOS 3 with Canon 600mm Af f/4 lens and 1.4x teleconverter; Fuji Velvia pushed one stop

CUCKOOS, ROADRUNNERS and ANIS

Greater Roadrunner

The roadrunner came so close to my blind that I could barely focus, and at such an angle that I had to squeeze my head into the corner of my blind. I was surprised that I managed to get a sharp image.

First Place

Photographer: Sean Fitzgerald and Jeremy Woodhouse
Landowner: Roberto and Fran Yzaguirre

Canon EOS 1N-RS with Canon 600mm lens and 25mm and 12mm extension tubes; f/5.6 @ 1/60 sec.; Kodak E100VS

Greater Roadrunner

In the evening light, the roadrunner came down to a water hole to drink. Fortunately, he chose to drink with his head in one of the small patches of sunlight.

Third Place

Photographer: Sean Fitzgerald and Jeremy Woodhouse
Landowner: Roberto and Fran Yzaguirre

Canon EOS 1N-RS with Canon 300mm f/2.8 lens and 2x teleconverter; f/8 @ 1/60 sec.; Kodak E100VS

Groove-billed Ani

Anis were plentiful and never wary. They spent much of their time in dense cover, like other cuckoos, but liked to sit in the open at first light. This one was on Granjeno foliage.

Second Place

Photographer: Cliff Beittel
Landowner: Frank D. Yturria – Yturria Ranch

Canon EOS 3 with Canon 600mm f/4L IS lens, 37mm extension and 1.4x teleconverter; f/5.6 @ 1/200 sec.; Fuji Provia F pushed one stop

JAYS, CROWS and RAVENS

Green Jay
I set up some tree stumps in a rain-fed pond and was rewarded with a jay checking out the area just after sunrise.
First Place
Photographer: David Welling
Landowner: Pérez Ranch – Rancho San Francisco

Nikon F5S with Nikon 500 F4S-AF-S lens and TC-20E 2x teleconverter; f/8 @ 1/60 sec.; Fuji Velvia pushed one stop

Green Jay
Three Green Jays continually visited a small pond and I was able to photograph them on several occasions. I liked the composition because it seemed to reflect the jay's notoriously curious nature.
Second Place
Photographer: David Welling
Landowner: Pérez Ranch – Rancho San Francisco

Nikon F5S with Nikon 500 F4-AF-S lens and TC-14E
1.4x teleconverter; f/5.6 @ 1/125 sec. with fill flash – Nikon SB28;
Fuji Velvia pushed one stop

Green Jay
We tried everything to get the bird to perch on this particular limb. Something finally worked—dog food!
Third Place
Photographer: Joseph Holman and Wallace Prukop
Landowner: Wallace Prukop

Canon EOS 1 with Canon 500mm f/4 lens; Fuji Velvia

SWALLOWS, NIGHTJARS and SWIFTS

‹ **Common Nighthawk**
The photo demonstrates the advantage of working with a knowledgeable landowner. I told her we needed nighthawks for one category. She led me out into the driveway to the ranch and pointed to a branch. A nighthawk roosted there every day. Standing in the back of a pickup truck allowed me to photograph at eye level.
First Place
Photographer: David Welling
Landowner: Pérez Ranch – Rancho San Francisco

Nikon F5S with Nikon 500 f/4-AF-S lens and TC-14E 1.4x teleconverter; f/5.6 @ 1/125 sec. with fill flash - Nikon SB28; Fuji Velvia pushed one stop

Common Nighthawk *(Top Right)*
One of the ponds of the ranch seemed to attract both insects and the nighthawks that prey upon them. The erratic flight of the nighthawks posed somewhat of a problem but added to the interest as well.
Second Place
Photographer: John D. and Adrienne Ingram
Landowner: Daniel Y. Butler – H. Yturria Land and Cattle

Nikon f5 with Nikon 500mm f/4 lens; f/4 @ 1/640 sec.; Fuji Provia

Lesser Nighthawk
I photographed the nighthawk over a several-week period as she nested along a caliche ridge.
Third Place
Photographer: Randall Ennis
Landowner: Baldo Jr. and Daniel Vela – San Pedro Ranch

Canon A2E with Canon 300mm 2.8 L lens and 2x teleconverter; f/11 @ 1/125 sec.; Fuji Sensia 100

TURKEYS, QUAIL and CHACHALACAS

< Northern Bobwhite
While I was working from a water-blind, photographing songbirds at the water's edge, a Northern Bobwhite came foraging for the deer corn I had laid down around the shore. The low angle of the shot helps to draw the viewer into the quail's environment.

First Place
Photographer: Sean Fitzgerald and Jeremy Woodhouse
Landowner: Roberto and Fran Yzaguirre

Canon EOS 3 with Canon EF 600mm f/4 lens; f/4 @ 1/350 sec.; Kodak E100VS

Wild Turkey
Turkeys aren't hunted on the ranch, and huge flocks emerge from the live oaks in the morning. This one, though, was strutting for a lone hen late in the afternoon, long after the others had headed back to cover.

Second Place
Photographer: Cliff Beittel
Landowner: Frank D. Yturria – Yturria Ranch

Canon EOS3 with Canon 600mm f/4L IS lens and 2x teleconverter; f/8; Fuji Provia F pushed one stop

Northern Bobwhite
I was sitting in my truck trying to photograph a Common Nighthawk when I saw a female Northern Bobwhite walking through the grass nearby. The wind was blowing strongly, and here is the only image I got in which the bird was not obscured by blowing grass.

Third Place
Photographer: Larry Ditto and Greg Lasley
Landowner: Bud and Jimmy Payne

Canon EOS3 with Canon EF 600mm f4 lens and 1.4x teleconverter; f/5.6 @ 1/125 sec.; Fuji Velvia pushed one stop

DOVES and RED-BILLED PIGEONS

‹ **Common Ground-Dove**
To obtain this water-level shot, I dug an enormous 1000-gallon pool which enabled me to lie in the water with my lens only one inch above the water's surface and come away with a dramatic image.

First Place
Photographer: Derrick Hamrick and Roberta E. Summers
Landowner: Jim and Kathy Collins and Carolyn Cook Landrum – Cook Ranch Properties

Canon EOS3 with Canon 400 2.8 IS lens; f/5.6 @ 1/250 sec.; Fuji Sensia 100

White-winged Dove
While I was waiting for mammals to come to water, these two doves landed on a nearby limb. I was not expecting them, but I have always said that you have to be there to get the photos. A little luck helps sometimes. You never know what will happen.

Second Place
Photographer: Bill Draker and Glenn Hayes
Landowner: Dr. Gary M. Schwarz, Dr. Steve Shepard and Partners – Tecomate Ranch

Canon EOS 3 with Canon 500mm f/4 IS lens and 1.4x teleconverter; f/11 @ 1/125 sec.; Fuji Sensia 100

Mourning Dove
The photo was shot late in the day with the steeply sloping light of the evening sun modeling its feathers.

Third Place
Photographer: John D. and Adrienne Ingram
Landowner: Daniel Y. Butler – H. Yturria Land and Cattle

Canon EOS 1V with Canon 500mm f/4 lens and 2x teleconverter; f/16 @ 1/60 sec.; Fuji Provia

WARBLERS, VIREOS and KINGLETS

< Cactus Wren
Cactus Wrens build bulky nests among the spines of a cactus or thorny bush. The other partner
will sing from a nearby perch.
First Place
Photographer: David Powell and Don Pederson
Landowner: Judge and Mrs. William Mallet – The Mary B. Ranch

Nikon F5 with Nikon 500mm f/4 AFS lens; f/5.6 @ 1/250 sec. with window mount; Kodak E100VS

Orange-crowned Warbler
This little guy visited my special water hole every
day for about a week for his morning bath.
Third Place
Photographer: David Welling
Landowner: Pérez Ranch – Rancho San Francisco

*Nikon f5S with Nikon 500F4-AF-S lens and
TC-2DE 2x teleconverter; f/5.6 @ 1/125 sec. with
fill flash - SB28; Fuji Velvia pushed one stop*

Yellow Warbler
It is extremely hard to get good portraits of the
diminutive Yellow Warbler. When this one settled
on a nearby tree limb, I was charmed by the
composition and the softness of the background.
Second Place
Photographer: Sean Fitzgerald and
Jeremy Woodhouse
Landowner: Roberto and Fran Yzaguirre

*Canon EOS 3 with Canon EF 600mm
f/4 lens and 1.4x teleconverter;
f/5.6 @ 1/250 sec.; Kodak E100VS*

MOCKINGBIRDS and THRASHERS

Curve-billed Thrasher
South Texas is spectacular in the spring when the brush is blooming.
The Curve-billed Thrasher is sitting on a blooming Guayacan bush
in early morning light.
First Place
Photographer: Bill Draker and Glenn Hayes
Landowner: Dr. Gary M. Schwarz, Dr. Steve Shepard and
Partners – Tecomate Ranch

*Canon EOS 3 with Canon 500mm f/4x IS lens and
1.4x teleconverter; Fuji Sensia 100*

Long-billed Thrasher

This thrasher, in an unusual pose, is not actually looking for guidance from above but at the berries above its perch. Thrashers are very active, and they can be aggressive toward other birds as well.

Second Place

Photographer: John English
Landowner: Benito and Toni Treviño – Rancho Lomitas Native Plant Nursery

Canon EOS-1N with Canon EF 100-400m f/4.5 - 5.6L IS lens; f/8 @ 1/500 sec.; Fuji Sensia II 100

Northern Mockingbird

Birds in general are captivating and interesting creatures. Their unique beauty, their songs and their ability to fly are a constant source of inspiration as well as a fascination.

Third Place

Photographer: Dominique and Dwight Chamberlain
Landowner: Calvin Bentsen – La Coma Ranch

Nikon f5 with Nikon 600mm f/4 lens, extension tube PK 13 and 1.4x teleconverter; 1/80 sec.; Fuji Provia 100F

BUNTINGS, GROSBEAKS and DICKCISSELS

‹ Painted Bunting

Each afternoon I was treated to displays of drinking and bathing by these beautiful Painted Buntings. On a particularly balmy and still afternoon, a bird just sat in the lukewarm water, casting a perfect reflection.

First Place
(First Place: Birds Division)
Photographer: Sean Fitzgerald and Jeremy Woodhouse
Landowner: Roberto and Fran Yzaguirre

Canon EOS 1V with Canon EF 600mm f/4 lens and 1.4x teleconverter; f/5.6 @ 1/250 sec.; Kodak E100VS

Painted Bunting
After I had spent many hours on the floor of a blind next to a water hole, a Painted Bunting dipped her body in the water. When she resurfaced, a large drop of water stayed on her head just long enough for me to capture the image.

Second Place
Photographer: Ruth Hoyt
Landowner: Guerra Brothers

Canon 1V-HS with Canon 100-400mm f/4.5-5.6 IS lens; f/5.6; Kodak E100VS

Dickcissel
Dickcissels were a real treat at the Yturria Ranch. This male liked to sing from a particular low mesquite. To photograph him, I drove through brush as high as the hood of my Jeep.

Third Place
Photographer: Cliff Beittel
Landowner: Frank D. Yturria – Yturria Ranch

Canon EOS 3 with Canon 600mm f/4L IS lens, 37mm extension and 1.4x teleconverter; f/5.6 @ 1/250 sec.; Fuji Velvia pushed one stop

CARDINALS and PYRRHULOXIAS

Northern Cardinal
Cardinals are one of my favorite birds to photograph. Trying to get birds to land in the right spots sometimes is hard, and when one does you have to be ready. This one did well.

First Place
(Third Place: Birds Division)
Photographer: Bill Draker and Glenn Hayes
Landowner: Dr. Gary M. Schwarz, Dr. Steve Shepard and Partners – Tecomate Ranch

Canon EOS3 with Canon 500mm f/4 IS lens and 1.4x teleconverter; f/14 @ 1/125 sec.; Fuji Sensia 100

Northern Cardinal

Less flamboyantly colored than her brilliant red mate, the female Northern Cardinal is nonetheless a lovely bird. Here she stretches for a drink from an ephemeral rain pool while clinging tightly to a branch.

Third Place

Photographer: Robert L. Stanley
Landowner: Carlos H. Cantu – Cantu Ranch

Nikon N70 with Nikon 500mm f/4 lens; f/4 @ 1/125 sec.; Fuji Velvia

Pyrrhuloxia

I created a small water hole and planted some Opuntia pads for greenery and background. The Opuntias surprised me by blooming profusely in March, providing beautiful contrasts to the bird life that visited the pond.

Second Place

Photographer: David Welling
Landowner: Pérez Ranch – Rancho San Francisco

Nikon F5S with Nikon 500 f/4-AF-S lens and TC-14E 1.4x teleconverter; f/5.6 @ 1/60 sec. with fill flash - SB28; Fuji Velvia pushed one stop

SPARROWS and TOWHEES

White-crowned Sparrow

I like to do as many photos as possible with natural light. There were not many days with good light, so I had to make every one count. With many different birds coming to the feeder, a great variety of species was photographed on the same day. This sparrow was one.

First Place

Photographer: Bill Draker and Glenn Hayes
Landowner: Dr. Gary M. Schwarz, Dr. Steve Shepard and Partners – Tecomate Ranch

Canon EOS 3 with Canon 500mm f/4 IS lens and 1.4x teleconverter; f/14 @ 1/125 sec.; Fuji Sensia 100

White-crowned Sparrow

Shots of bathing birds are always difficult because the little guys move so fast, thrashing about to get the water worked into their feathers. I got this eye level shot by using my pickup truck as a screen or blind, crawling onto the ground and shooting under it. It took several tries at a slow shutter speed to capture the thrashing wings, flying water droplets and motionless head.

Second Place
Photographer: Larry Ditto and Greg Lasley
Landowner: Bud and Jimmy Payne

Canon EOS 1N with Canon 300mm AF f/2.8 lens and 2x teleconverter; f/5.6 @ 1/125 sec.; Fuji Velvia pushed one stop

White-crowned Sparrow

While I was trying to photograph cardinals from my blind in blooming Huisachillo, a young sparrow lighted in a great spot and stayed a few seconds longer than normal. No other bird landed on the branch the rest of the morning!

Third Place
Photographer: Lee Kline
Landowner: Jim and Kathy Collins and Carolyn Cook Landrum – Cook Ranch Properties

Canon EOS 3 with Canon EF 600 F/4L lens and extension tube; Fuji Velvia @ ISO 40

ALL OTHER BIRDS

‹ Golden-fronted Woodpecker
When this male landed at the flower and started feeding, I almost didn't take the photograph because I was so surprised. Fortunately, my trigger finger is trained to act independently of my brain.

First Place
Photographer: David Welling
Landowner: Pérez Ranch – Rancho San Francisco

Nikon F5S with Nikon 500 F4-AF-S lens and TX-14E 1.4x AF teleconverter; f/5.6 @ 1/125 sec. with fill flash - SB280; Fuji Velvia pushed one stop

Ladder-backed Woodpecker
Compared to Golden-fronted Woodpeckers, Ladder-backs have been even harder for me to photograph. When a brightly colored male landed at my little pond, I could have kissed him. Instead, I managed about four shots before he left. He must have figured out my improper intentions since he never returned.

Second Place
Photographer: David Welling
Landowner: Pérez Ranch – Rancho San Francisco

Nikon F5S with Nikon 500 F4-AF-S lens and TX-14E 1.4x AF teleconverter; f/8 @ 1/125 sec.; Fuji Velvia pushed one stop

Golden-fronted Woodpecker
It is said that all the colors known to humans appear in fish. This must also be true of birds. I noticed several times during the contest all the different colors of birds around my feeder and around the water hole.

Third Place
Photographer: Bill Draker and Glenn Hayes
Landowner: Dr. Gary M. Schwarz, Dr. Steve Shepard and Partners – Tecomate Ranch

Canon EOS 3 with Canon 500mm f/4 IS and 1.4x teleconverter; f/11 @ 1/125 sec.; Fuji Sensia

FOURTH & FIFTH PLACE WINNERS

Great Blue Heron
On a cool overcast morning, I was treated to a marvelous show as the Great Blue hunted for Rio Grande Leopard Frogs. I believe that the soft light and the resulting slow shutter speed enhance the image.
Fourth Place
Category: Wading Birds
Photographer: Sean Fitzgerald and Jeremy Woodhouse
Landowner: Roberto and Fran Yzaguirre

Canon EOS 1V with EF 600 f/4 lens; f/4 @ 1/30 sec.; Kodak E100VS

Black-Bellied Whistling-Duck
A pair of Black-Bellied Whistling-Ducks was among a group of a dozen or so which I had been photographing for about two hours from the edge of a large pond. I was concealed in a Rue photo blind. These two separated from the others and swam to a log where, each resting upon one leg, they closed their eyes and seemed to go to sleep.
Fifth Place
Category: Waterfowl
Photographer: Bill Caskey and Omar Garcia
Landowner: Schaleben Interests

Nikon F5 with Nikon 500mm f/4 lens and TC-14B teleconverter; f/5.6 @ 1/60 sec.; Kodak E100VS

Ruby-throated Hummingbird
The hummingbirds were only around for about two weeks before they migrated north. I set up a perch close to the feeder and hoped one would land on it. I balanced the sunlight with my flash to get a good exposure on both the bird and the background.
Fifth Place
Category: Hummingbirds
Photographer: Bill Draker and Glenn Hayes
Landowner: Dr. Gary M. Schwarz, Dr. Steve Shepard and Partners – Tecomate Ranch

Canon EOS 1N with 70-200mm f/2.8 lens and 550 EZ flash; f/4 @ 1/250 sec.; Fuji Sensia

Brown-crested Flycatcher
A busy pair of adult Brown-crested Flycatchers was actively feeding young in a nest in a hollow stump. One of the adults came to the nest with an amazing variety of food items, including this butterfly.
Fourth Place
Category: Flycatchers and Kingbirds
Photographer: Larry Ditto and Greg Lasley
Landowner: Bud and Jimmy Payne

Canon EOS 3 with Canon EF 600mm f/4 and 1.4x teleconverter; f/5.6 @ 1/250 sec.; Fuji Velvia pushed one stop

American Coot and Red-eared Turtle

The Red-eared Turtle was reposing in the warm rays. An American Coot approached, beckoning the turtle to give up its spot. Finally the turtle moved away from badgering ol' coot. Thus, another fun day of life at the pond.

Fourth Place
Category: Rails, Gallinules and Coots
Photographer: Tom Urban
Landowner: King Ranch

Canon F1 with Canon FD 400mm 2.8L lens; f/4 @ 1/125 sec.; Fuji Velvia

Crested Caracara

The subject is preparing to fly off as another bird lands nearby.

Fourth Place
Category: Birds of Prey
Photographer: John Cancalosi
Landowner: Matt and Patty Gorges

Nikon F5 with Nikon 500 f/4 lens; f/5.6 @ 1/500 sec.; Fuji Velvia

Cattle Egret

In early May, these birds formed large flocks on the ranch but were hard to approach. While driving the dirt roads, I chanced upon a gathering and was able to fire off a series of shots as they took flight. By June, they were gone.

Fifth Place
Category: Wading Birds
Photographer: Ralph Paonessa
Landowner: Joe Michael Castellano – Castellano Ranch

Canon EOS 3 with Canon EF 100-400mm f/4.5-5.6 L lens; f/5.6 @ 1/1000 sec.; Ektachrome E100VS

American Coot

I was in awe over the stark beauty of the coot's bright red eye amidst its black plumage, the blue water and green background.

Fifth Place
Category: Rails, Gallinules and Coots
Photographer: Derrick Hamrick and Roberta E. Summers
Landowner: Jim and Kathy Collins and Carolyn Cook Landrum – Cook Ranch Properties

Canon EOS 3 with Canon 400mm f/2.8 IS lens and 2x teleconverter; f/5.6 @ 1/250 sec.; Fuji Sensia 100

Cinnamon Teal

Wearing a wet suit allowed me to tolerate March's cool water temperature. A low camera angle was very effective in capturing the Cinnamon Teal preening its feathers in the soft early morning light.

Fourth Place
Category: Waterfowl
Photographer: Derrick Hamrick and Roberta E. Summers
Landowner: Jim and Kathy Collins and Carolyn Cook Landrum – Cook Ranch Properties

Canon EOS 3 with Canon 400mm 2.8 IS lens and 2x teleconverter; f/5.6 @ 1/250 sec.; Fuji Sensia 100

Black-necked Stilt

Black-necked Stilts were present on ranch ponds for several weeks in the spring. During the period they fed heavily on invertebrates, constantly circling the edges of shallow ponds.

Fourth Place
Category: Shorebirds
Photographer: James Gift
Landowner: Harold and Maxine Turk – La Escondida Ranch

Nikon F5 with Nikon 600mm FS f/4 lens and TC-14E teleconverter; f5.6 @ 1/500 sec.; Fuji Provia F

Killdeer

Dozing in my blind in the mid-morning heat, I was awakened by the raucous call of this Killdeer as it flew to the water hole. It was one of a total of four shorebirds that I saw in the hot Texas interior during the whole contest.

Fifth Place
Category: Shorebirds
Photographer: Sean Fitzgerald and Jeremy Woodhouse
Landowner: Roberto and Fran Yzaguirre

Canon EOS3 with Canon EF 600 f/4 lens and 1.4x teleconverter; f/5.6 @ 1/350 sec.; Kodak E100VS

Scissor-tailed Flycather

During April, Scissor-tailed Flycatchers migrated through South Texas en masse. Photographing in grasslands with scattered clumps of brush provided many opportunities to "shoot" these birds on feeding perches. This early morning shot from the truck window caught a long-tailed adult bird just after it swallowed a bug.

Fifth Place
Category: Flycatchers and Kingbirds
Photographer: Larry Ditto and Greg Lasley
Landowner: Bud and Jimmy Payne

Canon EOS3 with Canon 600mm AF f/4 lens and 1.4x teleconverter; f6.3 @ 1/180 sec.; Fuji Velvia pushed one stop

Brown-headed Cowbird

A cowbird came to the feeder one morning when the sun was shining. During the times that the brush was blooming, I had very few days with good light.

Fifth Place
Category: Blackbirds, Orioles and Tanagers
Photographer: Bill Draker and Glenn Hayes
Landowner: Dr. Gary M. Schwarz, Dr. Steve Shepard and Partners – Tecomate Ranch

Canon EOS 3 with Canon 500mm f/4 IS lens and 1.4x teleconverter; f/13 @ 1/125 sec.; Fuji Sensia 100

Belted Kingfisher
Poised for launch, a Belted Kingfisher has her eye on a surface-feeding minnow. While surveying the pond with binoculars, I soon identified the kingfisher's favorite hunting perches. Gradually moving a blind closer to the snag over several days, I was able to photograph the bird at close range without disturbing her routine.

Fifth Place
Category: Kingfishers
Photographer: Larry Ditto and Greg Lasley
Landowner: Bud and Jimmy Payne

Canon EOS 3 with Canon 600mm AF f/4 lens and 1.4 x teleconverter; f/6.3 @ 1/80 sec.; Fuji Velvia pushed one stop

Great Horned Owl
While lying concealed on top of my van, I gave my assistant instructions via portable radio on how best to position the mobile elevated blind for a close-up of this incubating Great Horned Owl. The two young hatched and fledged successfully.

Fifth Place
Category: Birds of Prey
Photographer: Derrick Hamrick and Roberta E. Summers
Landowner: Jim and Kathy Collins and Carolyn Cook Landrum – Cook Ranch Properties

Canon EOS 3 with Canon 400mm f/2.8 IS lens and 2x teleconverter; f/6.3 @ 1/200 sec. with fill flash; Fuji Sensia 100

Belted Kingfisher
Our ranch was not noted for having many of these wonderful fish-eating birds. While sitting in a photo blind the previous day, I observed a female come in and land on a distant branch. Unfortunately, I had no shot. The next day I lucked out, for she landed on the closest snag to my blind!

Fourth Place
Category: Kingfishers
Photographer: Michael Francis and Mark S. Werner
Landowner: McAllen Properties

Canon EOS 1N with Canon 500mm lens; Fuji Sensia 100

Greater Roadrunner
A Greater Roadrunner and her mate nested near the Payne Ranch house. During frequent hunting forays, they would pause to investigate the photographer's comings and goings and pose for photos. In moments of curiosity or excitement, roadrunners exhibit an unfeathered red, white and blue skin patch behind the eye. A rather patriotic gesture, don't you think?

Fourth Place
Category: Cuckoos, Roadrunners and Anis
Photographer: Larry Ditto and Greg Lasley
Landowner: Bud and Jimmy Payne

Canon EOS 1N with Canon 300mm f/2.8 lens and 2x teleconverter; f/5.6 @ 1/500 sec.; Fuji Velvia pushed one stop

Ruby-throated Hummingbird

Betty Pérez told me they had hummingbirds hanging around the ranch house. I stayed there one day, set up a hummingbird feeder, and spent an afternoon watching these little dynamos feed and fight.

Fourth Place
Category: Hummingbirds
Photographer: David Welling
Landowner: Pérez Ranch – Rancho San Francisco

Nikon F5S with Nikon 500 F4-AF-S lens; f/5.4 @ 1/250 sec. with fill flash - Nikon SB28; Fuji Velvia pushed one stop

Green Jay

In early January, a beautiful rain-swollen pond proved a great photo location for a variety of birds. A pair of Green Jays would land on this tall stump every morning about sunrise. One morning the light was right, the Photo God smiled, and this jay cooperated.

Fourth Place
Category: Jays, Crows and Ravens
Photographer: David Welling
Landowner: Pérez Ranch – Rancho San Francisco

Nikon-F5S with Nikon 500F4-AF-S lens and TC-14E 1.4x teleconverter; f/5.6 @ 1/125 sec.; Fuji Velvia pushed one stop

Green Jay

A gorgeous resident of the Rio Grande Valley, the Green Jay is a true South Texas treasure. Commonly found at woodland deer feeders, the colorful and boisterous jay is easy to locate but difficult, at times, to properly photograph in revealing good light.

Fifth Place
Category: Jays, Crows and Ravens
Photographer: Mike Kelly
Landowner: J.A. Jr. and Sue Ann Garcia – Garcia Ranch

Nikon F5 with Nikon AF-S ED 600mm f/4 D IF lens and TC-14E teleconverter; f/8 @ 1/250 sec.; Fuji Velvia pushed one stop

Greater Roadrunner

The photograph was taken as the bird stepped into an opening, probably carrying the lizard to a nest hidden in the nearby brush. The bird seemed to carry prey items across this opening regularly, but it was very aware of the photographer's presence. By never going directly to the nest, the roadrunner was successful at keeping its location a secret.

Fifth Place
Category: Cuckoos, Roadrunners and Anis
Photographer: Tim Cooper and Mike Kryzwonski
Landowner: Harry Cullen – Buena Vista Ranch

Canon EOS 3 with Canon 600mm f/4 lens; f/5.6 @ 1/500 sec.; Fuji Provia F

Lesser Nighthawk

I was tracking a squirrel when it ran through the tree and suddenly startled the sleeping nighthawk. The bird was so well camouflaged, I hadn't seen it. I captured the image as it spread its wings, regaining its balance.

Fourth Place
Category: Swallows, Nightjars and Swifts
Photographer: Fred LaBounty
Landowner: Bert and Trudy Forthuber – Krenmueller Farms

Canon EOS 3 with Canon EF 500 f.4 L IS lens and EF 2x teleconverter; f/8 @ 1/30 sec.; Fuji Velvia rated at 40 ISO

Common Nighthawk

Nighthawks usually rest during the daylight hours and forage for insects at dusk and dawn. In late afternoon light, this one is keeping an eye open for a meal.

Fifth Place
Category: Swallows, Nightjars and Swifts
Photographer: David Powell and Don Pederson
Landowner: Judge and Mrs. William Mallet – The Mary B. Ranch

Nikon F5 with Nikon 500mm f/4 AFS lens and TC-14E teleconverter; f/4 @ 1/250 sec. with window mount; Kodak E100VS

Northern Bobwhite

A pair of quail started coming to my water hole in the afternoon for a refreshing drink. It took some time before I had the opportunity to frame these two lovebirds together for a nice ground-level portrait.

Fourth Place
Category: Turkeys, Quail and Chachalacas
Photographer: Derrick Hamrick and Roberta E. Summers
Landowner: Jim and Kathy Collins and Carolyn Cook Landrum – Cook Ranch Properties

Canon EOS 3 with Canon 400mm f/2.8 IS lens; f/5.6 @ 1/500 sec.; Fuji Sensia 100

Wild Turkey

The regal presence of a strutting gobbler attracts not only the attention of hens but nature enthusiasts as well. The resplendent iridescence of his plumage competes with the springtime colors of wildflowers.

Fifth Place

Category: Turkeys, Quail and Chachalacas
Photographer: Tom Urban
Landowner: King Ranch

Canon F1 with Canon FD 400mm f/2.8L lens; f/2.8 @ 1/125 sec.; Fuji Velvia

Mourning Dove

With my blind in the water and my camera inches above the water, I observed the dove nervously approaching the water to drink. I managed one or two shots before it flew away.

Fourth Place

Category: Doves and Red-billed Pigeons
Photographer: Sean Fitzgerald and Jeremy Woodhouse
Landowner: Roberto and Fran Yzaguirre

Canon EOS 1N-RS with Canon 600mm lens and 1.4x teleconverter; f/5.6 @ 1/125 sec.; Kodak E100VS

Common Ground-Dove

I was preparing to leave for the evening when a pair of Common Ground-Doves shyly approached the water. I made the shot and the left bird turned away, changing the composition to one that no longer worked.

Fifth Place

Category: Doves and Red-billed Pigeons
Photographer: Ruth Hoyt
Landowner: Guerra Brothers

Canon 1V-HS with Canon Ef 100-400mm f/4.5-5.6 L IS lens; f/5.6; Fuji Provia 100F pushed one stop

Bullock's Oriole

I had the photo blind at a small pond with water supplied from a drip system. The pond overflowed slightly and just as I was cursing the failure of technology, this beautiful oriole stopped at the overflow to bathe. I stopped cursing and kept the overflow going.

Fourth Place

Category: Blackbirds, Orioles and Tanagers
Photographer: David Welling
Landowner: Pérez Ranch – Rancho San Francisco

Nikon F5S with Nikon 500 F4-AF-S lens and TC-20E teleconverter; f/5 @ 1/125 sec. with fill flash - SB28; Fuji Velvia pushed one stop

Blue-gray Gnatcatcher

This little gnatcatcher was one of the many birds added to my life list, both seeing and photographing for the first time during the contest – an awesome experience.

Fifth Place
Category: Warblers, Vireos and Kinglets
Photographer: Kermit Denver Laird
Landowner: Juanita Farley – Speer Ranch

Nikon F5 with Nikkor 600mm f/4 AF-S lens and TC-14E 1.4x teleconverter; f/5.6 @ 1/250 sec.; Kodak Ektachrome E100VS

Curve-billed Thrasher

There were times when I had 20 to 25 different species of birds around my feeder. It was fun just to watch as they ate gallons of grain each day. This Curve-billed Thrasher was one.

Fourth Place
Category: Mockingbirds and Thrashers
Photographer: Bill Draker and Glenn Hayes
Landowner: Dr. Gary M. Schwarz, Dr. Steve Shepard and Partners – Tecomate Ranch

Canon EOS 3 with Canon 500mm f/4 IS lens and 1.4x teleconverter; f/11 @ 1/125 sec.; Fuji Sensia 100

Blue-gray Gnatcatcher

I was working from a beanbag in my truck as a small flock of birds foraged in some nearby mesquites. The gnatcatcher was tiny, but I decided to try a long lens and teleconverter for magnification and got lucky with a few shots.

Fourth Place
Category: Warblers, Vireos and Kinglets
Photographer: Larry Ditto and Greg Lasley
Landowner: Bud and Jimmy Payne

Canon EOS 3 with Canon EF 600mm f/4 lens, 2x teleconverter and 25mm extension tube; f/8 @ 1/125 sec.; Fuji Velvia pushed one stop

Gray Catbird

Gray Catbirds prefer thick brushy habitats and are fairly common in South Texas during spring and fall migration. The shot was taken from a blind placed almost at minimum focus distance to a small water hole where many small birds and other wildlife were coming to bathe and drink.

Fifth Place

Category: Mockingbirds and Thrashers
Photographer: Larry Ditto and Greg Lasley
Landowner: Bud and Jimmy Payne

Canon EOS 3 with Canon 300mm AF 2.8f lens and 2x teleconverter; f5.6 @ 1/250 sec.; Fuji Velvia pushed one stop

Painted Bunting

I had two Painted Buntings on the ground and this one perched on a Blackbrush branch at my "Outdoor Studio." I took more than eight frames of this particular bird and used manual mode on all frames.

Fourth Place

Category: Buntings, Grosbeaks and Dickcissels
Photographer: Pete and Mary L. Garcia
Landowner: Guerra Brothers

Minolta Maxxum 800si with Sigma 300 f/4 APO telephoto lens and 1.4x APO teleconverter; f/22 @ 1/15 sec.; Fuji Velvia

Painted Bunting

This water hole had dried up until a brief rain brought new life. I was afraid birds would not like the broken stick, but this bunting was only one of about 10 birds of four different species to stop almost exactly at this spot, survey the scene and embark on a leisurely bath.

Fifth Place

Category: Buntings, Grosbeaks and Dickcissels
Photographer: David Welling
Landowner: Pérez Ranch – Rancho San Francisco

Nikon F5S with Nikon 500mm F4-AF-S lens and TC-30E teleconverter; f/8 @ 1/125 sec.; Fuji Velvia pushed one stop

Northern Cardinal

There were so many opportunities to photograph cardinals in the area that I took too many and therefore had a problem choosing one to enter.

Fourth Place
Category: Cardinals and Pyrrhuloxias
Photographer: Bill Burns
Landowner: Bill Burns – Burns Ranch

Canon EOS 3 with Canon 500mm IS lens; f/5.6 @ 1/250 sec.; Kodak E100VS

Botteri's Sparrow

On the Yturria Ranch, Botteri's Sparrows almost completely displace the closely related Cassin's Sparrows I photographed in 1998, just 35 miles farther west. This male sang tirelessly from an isolated brush pile amid acres of grass.

Fourth Place
Category: Sparrows and Towhees
Photographer: Cliff Beittel
Landowner: Frank D. Yturria – Yturria Ranch

Canon EOS 3 with Canon 600mm f/4L IS lens, 37mm extension and 1.4x teleconverter; f/8 @ 1/250 sec.; Fuji Velvia pushed one stop

Northern Cardinal

It was always fun when the cardinals arrived for their daily bath. They were aggressive toward other bird species at the water hole, chasing them off before washing up in private!

Fifth Place
Category: Cardinals and Pyrrhuloxias
Photographer: Michael Francis and Mark Werner
Landowner: McAllen Properties

Canon EOS 1N with Canon 500mm lens; Fuji Sensia 100

White-crowned Sparrow
Blackbrush is very pretty when it is blooming, but it is hard to get birds to land on it in exactly the right place at the right time.
Fifth Place
Category: Sparrows and Towhees
Photographer: Bill Draker and Glenn Hayes
Landowner: Dr. Gary M. Schwarz, Dr. Steve Shepard and Partners – Tecomate Ranch

Canon EOS 3 with Canon 500mm f/4 IS lens and 1.4x teleconverter; f/13 @ 1/125 sec.; Fuji Sensia 100

Golden-fronted Woodpecker
This bird and his mate were feeding young, one adult arriving every minute or so with insects or berries. The nest was shaded most of the day but got direct sun for two hours before sunset.
Fourth Place
Category: All Other Birds
Photographer: Cliff Beittel
Landowner: Frank D. Yturria – Yturria Ranch

Canon EOS 3 with Canon 600mm f/4L lens, 25mm extension and 2x teleconverter; f/11 @ 1/90 sec.; Fuji Provia F pushed one stop

Golden-fronted Woodpecker
A male was flying back and forth to the nest along with the female as they fed a single offspring. They brought everything in for their new youngster from grasshoppers to berries. A mushy worm seemed to photograph best.
Fifth Place
Category: All Other Birds
Photographer: Joseph Holman and Wallace Prukop
Landowner: Wallace Prukop

Canon EOS 1 with Canon 300mm f/2.8 lens and #25 extension tube; Fuji Velvia

Cliff Beittel/Frank D. Yturria

Tom Urban/King Ranch

Derrick Hamrick and Roberta E. Summers/
Jim and Kathy Collins and Carolyn Cook Landrum

Michael Francis and Mark S. Werner/McAllen Properties

Sean Fitzgerald and Jeremy Woodhouse/
Roberto and Fran Yzaguirre

Ruth Hoyt/Guerra Brothers

Linda Peterson/Joe E. Chapa

Michael Francis and Mark S. Werner/McAllen Properties

MAMMALS

We have respect for the animals. We don't keep them in cages or torture them. We know that the animal is a spirit. It is not just an animal. It is more than that.

— a Hopi hunter

*Sean Fitzgerald and Jeremy Woodhouse/
Roberto and Fran Yzaguirre*

I learned to appreciate nature at an early age. My earliest memories are of trips with my dad and brothers to fish the Laguna Madre. Later, we enjoyed the King Ranch through permits my dad was able to get. I remember the Wild Turkey gobblers parading in the spring sunshine and herds of White-tailed Deer and Javelinas.

By the time I was seven, I recall sitting under an enormous mesquite tree in a vacant lot behind our house in Kingsville, bundled up against the cold of a "blue norther." I watched in amazement as tiny birds, kinglets, gnatcatchers and warblers, came within a few feet of my nose. Hispid Cotton Rats and White-footed Mice would occasionally come right up to my shoes, sniffing with their trembling noses, and winning their way into my heart.

I was on my way to learning that all of South Texas has been endowed with a wonderful diversity of mammals: Nine-banded Armadillo, Virginia Opossum, Pocket Mouse, Bobcat, Collared Peccary, and myriad others. A friend from New Jersey, in school with me at Texas A&I University in Kingsville, once told me that when he arrived in South Texas, he did not think there would be any wildlife because the brushlands looked so stark and uninviting. To his amazement, he discovered an unimaginable diversity of mammals, birds, amphibians, reptiles and fish, all the vertebrate classes.

Whether admiring the magnificence of a White-tailed Deer with an imposing rack, or a pair of Ocelot kittens, snug in their nest, we humans are gifted with the ability to appreciate other life forms as can no other species. We are drawn to the conservation of these varied mammal species, because they do provide so many opportunities for wonder and appreciation, as well as play a role in our environment. We all know how bat populations keep insects in check and how Coyotes control rodents. Whether for their intrinsic value or for the role they play in ecology, mammals have certainly earned our respect.

The photographs on the following pages are intimate views into the world of mammals in South Texas. Many of these creatures are secretive, and the photographers had to use all of their wit and skill to capture these remarkable images. It is easy to see how something like a mouse or shrew can hide until dark, but larger mammals like feral hogs or deer are also adept at staying hidden whenever they want.

Just think of it—a class of animals that includes members who fly, members who defend themselves by means of chemical warfare, some adapted to live on dry land, and others in the seven seas. Turn the pages and look at these lifelike images. Appreciate the skills of the photographers, the willingness of ranchers to share their land for this contest and the very subjects themselves, the mammals, arrayed in all their splendid diversity.

Look with interest, joy and outright humor at this collection. They are the best of the best, showing the wonderful variety that sparked my friend's comments thirty years ago.

*Stephen Labuda Jr.
Brownsville, Texas*

Stephen Labuda Jr. is a U.S. Fish and Wildlife Service biologist who specializes in mammals. He is the Project Leader of the Laguna Atascosa National Wildlife Refuge.

DEER

White-tailed Deer
On a foggy spring morning an elegant buck appeared in a soft pastel
setting. The scene radiated serenity.
First Place
(Fourth Place: Mammals Division)
Photographer: Tom Urban
Landowner: King Ranch

Canon F1 with Canon 400mm 2.8L lens; f/2.8 @ 1/60sec.; Fuji Velvia

White-tailed Deer

It was late in the season, so these bucks were sparring halfheartedly. White-tails aren't hunted on the ranch, so getting close (much closer than this) was easy. Now I understand buck fever!

Second Place

Photographer: Cliff Beittel
Landowner: Frank D. Yturria – Yturria Ranch

Canon EOS 3 with Canon 600mm f/4L lens; f/4 @ 1/30 sec.;
Fuji Provia F pushed two stops

White-tailed Deer

The early morning fog hadn't lifted when the deer started coming out into the open to feed. With such poor light I decided to change films to gain an extra stop of speed for possible action shots. This deer heard the noise of my activity. It looked my way and proceeded to stomp the ground to warn others of a possible threat.

Third Place

Photographer: Tom Vezo
Landowner: Phil and Karen Hunke – El Tecolote Ranch

Nikon F5 with Nikon 600mm AFI-F-4 lens; f/8 @ 1/160 sec.;
Fuji Provia pushed to 200

JAVELINAS

Javelina (Collared Peccary)
Although Javelinas are usually fairly shy, this one was very intent on relieving the Prickly Pear of its succulent leaves. It eagerly consumed its nopalito "salad," thorns and all.

First Place
Photographer: Sean Fitzgerald and Jeremy Woodhouse
Landowner: Roberto and Fran Yzaguirre

Canon EOS 3 with Canon EF 600mm f/4 lens and 1.4x teleconverter; f/5.6 @ 1/125 sec.; Kodak E100VS

Javelina (Collared Peccary)

My first trip to South Texas was centered around this pond. White-tailed Deer, Great Kiskadees and these Javelinas seemed to live there. The evening light was only getting better and better when my subjects arrived to drink.

Second Place

Photographer: Michael Francis and Mark S. Werner
Landowner: McAllen Properties

Nikon F4 with Nikon 80-200mm f/2.8 lens; f/5.6 @ 1/250 sec.; Fuji Provia 100F

Javelina (Collared Peccary)

I had scattered feed corn in a clearing, trying to photograph a large White-tailed buck that was in the area, but to no avail. Two Javelinas showed up to eat my corn or to show off for the camera.

Third Place

Photographer: Bill Draker and Glenn Hayes
Landowner: Dr. Gary M. Schwarz, Dr. Steve Shepard and Partners – Tecomate Ranch

Canon EOS 3 with Canon 500mm f/4 IS lens; f/5.6 @ 1/125 sec.; Fuji Sensia 100

RODENTS

Eastern Fox Squirrel
While I was attempting to film songbirds on a perch near some blooming lantana, an Eastern Fox Squirrel appeared. Always resourceful endearing rodents, they will investigate wherever birds are feeding, hoping to find food for themselves.

First Place
Photographer: Tom Urban
Landowner: King Ranch

Canon F1 with Canon FD 400mm 2.8L lens;
f/5.6 @ 1/125 sec.; Fuji Velvia

Southern Plains Woodrat
Measuring some 20 inches in length, this healthy but hungry specimen is quite active at night. The woodrat made trip after trip into my camp, eating everything from birdseed to mesquite beans and cactus tuna.
Second Place
Photographer: John English
Landowner: Benito and Toni Treviño – Rancho Lomitas Native Plant Nursery

Canon EOS 1N with Canon EF 100mm f/2.8 macro lens; f/8 @ 1/250 sec. with remote flash; Fuji Sensia II 100

Eastern Fox Squirrel
It often appears that Eastern Fox Squirrels are either feeding or hunting for something to eat. I had a feeling of surrealism while filming this squirrel during a foggy sunrise.
Third Place
Photographer: Tom Urban
Landowner: King Ranch

Canon F1 with Canon FD 400mm 2.8L lens; f/2.8 @ 1/125 sec.; Fuji Velvia

RABBITS and HARES

Eastern Cottontail
A rabbit could be found from time to time in the yard of the home where I stayed. It was wild but approachable if movements were slow and one stayed low. I was able to come in close for a shot.
First Place
(First Place: Mammals Division)
Photographer: Derrick Hamrick and Roberta E. Summers
Landowner: Jim and Kathy Collins and Carolyn Cook Landrum –
Cook Ranch Properties

Canon EOS 3 with Canon 400mm 2.8 IS lens;
f/6.3 @ 1/125 sec. with fill flash; Fuji Sensia 100

Black-tailed Jackrabbit

In the last light of the day, I saw this guy by the side of the road. He froze as long as I stood but dashed off when I knelt to try for a low angle. I tried to turn and shoot as he darted away but only managed to get off just two good shots.

Second Place
Photographer: J. Stephen Lay
Landowner: Minten Ranch

Nikon F100 with Nikon 300mm f/4 lens; f/4 @ 1/30 sec.; Kodak E100VS shot @ 200

Eastern Cottontail

A rabbit was in the shade of a bush, chewing grass, so I opted to use a special flash to bring out the detail and allow light to emphasize the front paws at its mouth.

Third Place
Photographer: Derrick Hamrick and Roberta E. Summers
Landowner: Jim and Kathy Collins and Carolyn Cook Landrum – Cook Ranch Properties

Canon EOS 3 with Canon 400mm 2.8 IS lens;
f/6.3 @ 1/125 sec. with fill flash; Fuji Sensia 100

WILD CATS

‹ Bobcat
The Bobcat caught my approach to the blind and slipped into heavy cover. It took about an hour before he reappeared for a quick photo.

First Place
(Fifth Place: Mammals Division)
Photographer: Michael Francis and Mark S. Werner
Landowner: McAllen Properties

Canon EOS 3 with Canon 500mm lens and 1.4x teleconverter; f/6.3 @ 1/90 sec.; Kodak E100VS

Bobcat
The cat had appeared on several occasions prior to this, my last day to shoot for the contest. After sitting all day I was prepared for disappointment, when it finally appeared.

Second Place
Photographer: Michael Francis and Mark S. Werner
Landowner: McAllen Properties

Canon EOS 3 with Canon 500mm lens; f/6.3 @ 1/90 sec.; Kodak E100VS

Bobcat
Mama Bobcat brought her two babies in for a refreshing drink on a very hot summer day. Watching the cats interact within 15-20 feet of my blind was an exciting treat. To capture them on film was icing on the cake!

Third Place
Photographer: Laura Elaine Moore and Steve Bentsen
Landowner: McAllen Properties

Nikon F4 with Nikon 400mm f/3.5 lens, 1.4x teleconverter and tripod; Fuji Sensia

COYOTES and FOXES

⟨ Coyote

Every day a Coyote came to the water hole at around the same time. Any movement sent it scurrying back into the brush. I was able to get two frames in the warm afternoon light.

First Place
Photographer: Sean Fitzgerald and Jeremy Woodhouse
Landowner: Roberto and Fran Yzaguirre

Canon EOS 3 with Canon EF 600mm f/4 lens; f/4 @ 1/60 sec.; Kodak E100VS

Coyote *(Top Right)*
Like clockwork, these two boys appeared every morning to drink, look around, and be off again. The fog of a January morning offered a special effect.

Second Place
Photographer: Michael Francis and Mark S. Werner
Landowner: McAllen Properties

Nikon F4 with Nikon 500mm f/4 lens and 1.4x teleconverter; Fuji Sensia 100

Coyote
The female's attention was not toward the camera, but rather on two subordinate members of the pack feeding on the carcass that she and the male had just left.

Third Place
Photographer: J. Stephen Lay
Landowner: Minten Ranch

Nikon F5 with Nikon 600mm f/4 lens; f/8 @ 1/125 sec.; Kodachrome 200

ARMADILLOS

< **Nine-banded Armadillo**
It took considerable time to get close enough for a satisfactory shot. The armadillo seemed to have a knack for turning his back to the camera. I was seeking an image with his head covered with mud, but finally it was more interesting with his head deeply buried.
First Place
Photographer: John D. and Adrienne Ingram
Landowner: Daniel Y. Butler – H. Yturria Land and Cattle

Nikon F5 with Nikon 600mm f/4 lens; f/8 @ 1/250 sec.; Fuji Provia

Nine-banded Armadillo *(Top Right)*
Armadillos spend much of their time digging for food with their powerful claws. Occasionally, as in this case, I find them searching for food at water tanks.
Second Place
Photographer: Mike Kelly
Landowner: J.A. Jr. and Sue Ann Garcia – Garcia Ranch

Nikon F5 with Nikon AF-S ED 500 f/4 D-IF lens; f/8 @ 1/250 sec.; Fuji Velvia pushed one stop

Nine-banded Armadillo
The armadillo's poor sight and docile disposition allowed me to observe this fascinating creature in its evening pursuits. As the light faded, I moved upwind and caught the resulting pose.
Third Place
Photographer: Linda Peterson
Landowner: Joe E. Chapa

Canon EOS 3 with Canon 500mm f/4 IS lens; f/4.5 @ 1/30 sec.; Kodachrome 200

MUSTELIDS

‹ Striped Skunk
One evening I spied a Striped Skunk, anticipated where he was going and worked my way ahead. He caught sight of me and began trotting. I focused and shot one frame, forgetting to pan with the camera. I remembered on the second frame, and you see the results.

First Place
Photographer: Ruth Hoyt
Landowner: Guerra Brothers

Canon 1V-HS with Canon 100-400mm f/4.5-5.6 IS lens; f/5.6;
Fuji Provia 100F pushed to 200

Striped Skunk *(Top Right)*
This skunk almost drove me insane. After putting out bait and waiting night after night with fire ants literally eating holes in my tent floor, I tried to manually focus on a dark subject with dark eyes.

Second Place
Photographer: Derrick Hamrick and Roberta E. Summers
Landowner: Jim and Kathy Collins and Carolyn Cook Landrum –
Cook Ranch Properties

Canon EOS 3 with Canon 400mm 2.8 IS lens; f/8 @ 1/200 sec.; Fuji Sensia 100

Long-tailed Weasel
This beady-eyed, masked little fellow with a beautiful pink tongue, flowing fur and long tail ran past me. He was gone in seconds. "Man, what was that?" I exclaimed to my trusted assistant and photo partner.

Third Place
Photographer: Mary Jo Janovsky and Mary Donahue
Landowner: Mary Jo Janovsky and Mary Donahue – RGV Shooting Center

Canon EOS with Canon EF 300mm lens and EF 1.4x teleconverter;
f/5.6 @ 1/250 sec.; Fuji Velvia

RACCOONS, COATIS and RINGTAILS

Common Raccoon

I photographed the three young raccoons as they crawled on the branches of an old tree. They never stopped moving for a minute, and I only got off one shot with them in this position. (Yes, there are three.)

First Place
(Third Place: Mammals Division)

Photographer: Sean Fitzgerald and Jeremy Woodhouse
Landowner: Roberto and Fran Yzaguirre

Canon EOS 1N-RS with Canon 300mm lens;
f/8 @ 1/30 sec.; Kodak E100VS

Common Raccoon
One of the three young raccoons crawled up to a notch in a tree and briefly looked straight at me before scampering back to rejoin the others.
Third Place
Photographer: Sean Fitzgerald and Jeremy Woodhouse
Landowner: Roberto and Fran Yzaguirre

Canon EOS 1N-RS with Canon 300mm f/2.8 lens;
f/5.6 @ 1/60 sec.; Kodak E100VS

Common Raccoon
I think this raccoon got accustomed to me being around. I was sitting on the bank of the water hole when he came and ignored me. In fact, he sat down there too.
Second Place
Photographer: Bill Draker and Glenn Hayes
Landowner: Dr. Gary M. Schwarz, Dr. Steve Shepard and Partners –
Tecomate Ranch

Canon EOS 3 with Canon 500mm f/4 IS lens; f/11 @ 1/250 sec.; Fuji Sensia 100

ALL OTHER MAMMALS

< **Nilgai**

Because they are hunted, most of the ranch's many Nilgai were wary. For some reason, this buck wasn't. I photographed him over many weeks. The Bronzed Cowbird was picking ticks and other insects from his coat.

First Place
(Second Place: Mammals Division)
Photographer: Cliff Beittel
Landowner: Frank D. Yturria – Yturria Ranch

Canon EOS 3 with Canon 600mm f/4L lens; f/5.6 @ 1/100 sec.; Fuji Velvia pushed one stop

Virginia Opossum

The nocturnal opossum usually spends its time scavenging for something to eat. A whimsical little individual paused long enough to be photographed before scurrying off into the brush.

Third Place
Photographer: Bill Leidner
Landowner: John and Audrey Martin

Pentax LX with Vivitar 135mm f/2.8 macro lens; f/8 @ 1/60 sec.; Fuji Sensia II

Axis Deer

Axis Deer juveniles or does often nuzzle the bucks, apparently a form of subservient behavior. Such action may be important to affirm the dominance of males, since these deer travel in mixed herds including bucks, does and juveniles.

Second Place
Photographer: James Gift
Landowner: Harold and Maxine Turk – La Escondida Ranch

Nikon F5 with Nikon 600mm f/4 AFS lens; f/5.6 @ 1/500 sec.; Fuji Provia F

FOURTH & FIFTH PLACE WINNERS

White-tailed Deer
It was early morning light and a nice buck was backlighted in a field of Seacoast Bluestem Grass. Such a scene will always be imprinted in my memory even if I had not caught it on film.
Fourth Place
Category: Deer
Photographer: Tom Urban
Landowner: King Ranch

Canon F1 with Canon 400mm 2.8L lens; f/2.8 @ 1/125 sec.; Kodak E100VS

Javelina (Collared Peccary)
Many of the lower leaves of the nopal had been eaten already, so it was at a stretch that this Javelina was able to break off the remaining leaves. Although Javelinas do not have good eyesight, their sharp "tusks" are a warning to photographers against getting too close!
Fourth Place
Category: Javelinas
Photographer: Sean Fitzgerald and Jeremy Woodhouse
Landowner: Roberto and Fran Yzaguirre

Canon EOS 3 with Canon EF 600mm f/4 lens and 1.4x teleconverter; f/5.6 @ 1/125 sec.; Kodak E100VS

White-footed Mouse
These mice were a nuisance in the camp building on the ranch. I lured them to a miniature studio with sunflower seeds, where I was waiting for a macro portrait.
Fourth Place
Category: Rodents
Photographer: Ralph Paonessa
Landowner: Joe Michael Castellano – Castellano Ranch

Canon EOS 3 with Canon EF 180mm f/3.5L macro lens; f/11 @ 1/200 sec. with two Canon 550EX flashes; Fuji Velvia

Mexican Ground Squirrel
A fairly quiet morning, and I was starting to get really warm in the blind. Fortunately, the ground squirrel arrived to distract me from the uncomfortable conditions.
Fifth Place
Category: Rodents
Photographer: Sean Fitzgerald and Jeremy Woodhouse
Landowner: Roberto and Fran Yzaguirre

Canon EOS 3 with Canon EF 600mm f/4 lens and 1.4x teleconverter; f/5.6 @ 1/250 sec.; Kodak E100VS

White-tailed Deer

Here is a shot I knew was a winner as soon as I saw it. It captures the playful energy and grace of a yearling White-tailed Deer. The young fellow began leaping about as its mother and several other deer stood nearby. The photographer's vehicle is often the best photography blind since many species are accustomed to seeing the landowner's truck from day to day.

Fifth Place
Category: Deer
Photographer: Larry Ditto and Greg Lasley
Landowner: Bud and Jimmy Payne

Canon EOS 3 with Canon 600mm AF f/4 lens and 1.4x teleconverter; f/6.3 @ 1/250 sec.; Fuji Velvia pushed one stop

Javelina (Collared Peccary)

It is spring in South Texas and the vegetation is displaying a lush green coat of fresh leaves. A Javelina in the late light of day, with the springtime richness of new life, presents a picturesque scene of contrast.

Fifth Place
Category: Javelinas
Photographer: Tom Urban
Landowner: King Ranch

Canon F1 with Canon FD 400mm 2.8L lens; f/5.6 @ 1/125 sec.; Kodak E100VS

Black-tailed Jackrabbit

Wildlife photographers are always looking for displays of behavior by their subjects. When these jackrabbits nudged each other as if to say, "Don't just sit there eating; get up and chase me," the pursuit was on. Unfortunately, the chase proved more difficult to capture than the nose-rubbing that started it.

Fourth Place
Category: Rabbits and Hares
Photographer: Larry Ditto and Greg Lasley
Landowner: Bud and Jimmy Payne

Canon EOS 3 with Canon 300mm AF f/2.8 lens and 2x teleconverter; f/6.3 @ 1/250 sec.; Fuji Velvia pushed one stop

Black-tailed Jackrabbit
I found a small field where jackrabbits met every afternoon to talk and eat. One apparently had never seen a Jeep before. He gave my vehicle the strangest look, and I managed to capture it on film.
Fifth Place
Category: Rabbits and Hares
Photographer: David Welling
Landowner: Pérez Ranch – Rancho San Francisco

Nikon-F5S with Nikon 500mm f/4 AF-S lens and TC-14E 1.4x AF teleconverter; f/5.6 @ 1/125 sec. with window mount; Fuji Velvia pushed one stop

Bobcat
The Bobcat could sometimes be found dozing on a limb under the shade of a large mesquite tree. I approached the tree, knowing the cat would flee. Kneeling in the grass, I turned and fired as it bounded away.
Fourth Place
Category: Wild Cats
Photographer: Derrick Hamrick and Roberta E. Summers
Landowner: Jim and Kathy Collins and Carolyn Cook Landrum – Cook Ranch Properties

Canon EOS 1N-RS with Canon 100-400mm 5.6 IS lens; f/5.6 @ 1/125 sec.; Fuji Sensia 100

Bobcat
While making afternoon rounds to scent-mark his territory with a spray of urine, a tomcat strolled through my territory. His face was lionesque when he looked my way before ambling into a nearby thicket.
Fifth Place
Category: Wild Cats
Photographer: Larry Ditto and Greg Lasley
Landowner: Bud and Jimmy Payne

Canon EOS 3 with Canon 600mm AF f/4 lens and 1.4x teleconverter; f/6.3 @ 1/250 sec.; Fuji Velvia pushed one stop

Coyote

I had noticed Coyote tracks on a small trail to a watering hole, so I set up nearby and waited. In the soft dusk light, the Coyote finally came down. After drinking nervously, he briefly looked up through the brush.

Fifth Place
Category: Coyotes and Foxes
Photographer: Sean Fitzgerald and Jeremy Woodhouse
Landowner: Roberto and Fran Yzaguirre

Canon EOS 1N-RS with Canon 600mm; f/5.6 @ 1/60 sec.; Kodak E100VS

Nine-banded Armadillo

No species better symbolizes Texas, for me, than the armadillo. Here, one is out for an early morning forage.

Fourth Place
Category: Armadillos
Photographer: Mike Kelly
Landowner: J.A. Jr. and Sue Ann Garcia – Garcia Ranch

Nikon F5 with Nikon AF-S ED 500mm f/4 D-IF lens; f/8 @ 1/250 sec.; Fuji Velvia pushed one stop

Coyote

The healthy-looking Coyote had just drunk at the pond and was checking out what food it might find. It pawed and sniffed the ground but came up empty, marked the area and drifted quietly away.

Fourth Place
Category: Coyotes and Foxes
Photographer: Tom Urban
Landowner: King Ranch

Canon F1 with Canon 400mm 2.8L lens and FD 1.4x-A teleconverter; f/4 @ 1/250 sec.; Fuji Velvia

Common (Grant's) Zebra

The two adult zebras on the ranch were very protective of their offspring. Each time I tried to approach, the male would usher the mother and colt away. One day when my efforts were thwarted and I left the area, I noticed in my rearview mirror that the male actually followed me to make sure I didn't change my mind. One evening on my way back to camp, I encountered the mom and junior again. Preoccupied, they ignored me while I captured their touching exchange on film.

Fourth Place
Category: All Other Mammals
Photographer: Irene Sacilotto
Landowner: Daniel Y. Butler – H. Yturria Land & Cattle

Nikon F5 with Nikon 300mm f/2.8 lens; f/5.6 @ 1/400 sec.;
Fuji Sensia 100

American Badger

An early morning surprise! I heard rustling in the grass and got my camera gear ready to photograph what I figured would be a small Javelina or raccoon. Turns out it was the only sighting of a badger I had in the six-month photo shoot.

Fifth Place
Category: Mustelids
Photographer: Michael Francis and Mark S. Werner
Landowner: McAllen Properties

Canon EOS 1N with Canon 500mm lens; Kodachrome 200

Nine-banded Armadillo

Armadillos commonly feed in grass adjacent to native brush. This is a photograph from Roll 3, Day 1, the afternoon of January 17, 2000, following my midday arrival to begin the contest.

Fifth Place
Category: Armadillos
Photographer: Cliff Beittel
Landowner: Frank D. Yturria – Yturria Ranch

Canon EOS 3 with Canon 600mm f/4 L lens, 25mm extension and
1.4x teleconverter; f/8 @ 1/200 sec.; Fuji Velvia pushed one stop

Striped Skunk

Although several species of skunks occur in Texas, the Striped Skunk is by far the most frequently encountered. The handsome animal holds its bushy tail raised high as it ambles through the grass.

Fourth Place
Category: Mustelids
Photographer: Kevin and Shannon Vandivier
Landowner: Ana, Jaime and Leticia Tijerina – Caramacaro Ranch

(no technical information provided)

Common Raccoon

Life around the water hole was always interesting, with many critters coming during the time I was there. This raccoon was a regular, and I couldn't resist spending a little film every time he would give me a shot.

Fourth Place
Category: Raccoons, Coatis and Ringtails
Photographer: Bill Draker and Glenn Hayes
Landowner: Dr. Gary M. Schwarz, Dr. Steve Shepard and Partners – Tecomate Ranch

Canon EOS 3 with Canon 500mm f/4 IS lens; f/11 @ 1/250 sec.; Fuji Sensia 100

Common Raccoon

Circling the tank daily in an effort to catch fish, bugs, or anything else, a raccoon stopped just long enough for me to snap a few shots.

Fifth Place
Category: Raccoons, Coatis and Ringtails
Photographer: Bill Draker and Glenn Hayes
Landowner: Dr. Gary M. Schwarz, Dr. Steve Shepard and Partners – Tecomate Ranch

Canon EOS 3 with Canon 500mm f/4 IS lens and 1.4x teleconverter; f/16 @ 1/125 sec.; Fuji Sensia 100

Eland

I photographed this Eland from my vehicle, which I used as a mobile blind. Accustomed to seeing the ranch employees with similar vehicles, he tolerated my presence and allowed me to approach and turn off the engine. With what seemed to be curiosity, he calmly watched me from the protection of a clump of small trees.

Fifth Place
Category: All Other Mammals
Photographer: Irene Sacilotto
Landowner: Daniel Y. Butler – H. Yturria Land & Cattle

Nikon F5 with Nikon 600mm f/4 lens; f/4 @ 1/250 sec.; Fuji Sensia 100

David Welling/Pérez Ranch

John and Gloria Tveten/Rosemary and Cleve Breedlove

Ralph Paonessa/Joe Michael Castellano

John and Gloria Tveten/Rosemary and Cleve Breedlove

Michael Francis and Mark S. Werner/McAllen Properties

Joseph Holman and Wallace Prukop/Wallace Prukop

John D. and Adrienne Ingram/Bentsen Palm Development

Derrick Hamrick and Roberta E. Summers/
Jim and Kathy Collins and Carolyn Cook Landrum

INSECTS & ARACHNIDS

Nature will bear the closest inspection. She invites us to lay our eye level with her smallest leaf and take an insect view of its plain.

— Henry David Thoreau

Cliff Beittel/Frank D. Yturria

The noted Harvard scientist E.O. Wilson writes, "The diversity of life forms, so numerous that we have yet to identify most of them, is the greatest wonder of this planet."

Such diversity is evident here in South Texas in the treasure-trove of—among other flora and fauna—our insects. For example, over 800 species of beetles alone have been documented at the 500-acre Sabal Palm Grove Audubon Sanctuary in Brownsville. What fantastic entomofauna exists here and yet remains a mystery to most of us!

In 1995, an insect pitfall trap was set in our area for a mere 24-hour period. During that time, a large sapphire Blue Scarab Beetle (*Panaeus adonis*), never before documented in all of Texas, was collected. What other species are here just waiting to be discovered!

Why should we value diversity in the natural world, as so readily exemplified by insects? Capable as we are of destroying our world, we are obligated to learn more about any given ecosystem to determine its biological value.

Restoring diversity can be a lengthy and complicated process. Ethical use of the land and all of its components—soil, water, plants, and animals—should be based on respect for and love of nature by local people, rather than our reliance solely on government regulations. Management of wildlife corridors, such as ours in South Texas, must be based on good inventories of flora and fauna and related ecological conditions.

Tragically, very little is known about the invertebrates that reside in the Rio Grande Delta. Baseline data of these animals are needed in order to understand how to restore their habitat. Insects and arachnids are often overlooked when such data are collected, but they are actually the most important ingredient in the species mix.

Insects are fascinating creatures as well! For example, South Texas is the home of a species of long-horned wood-boring beetle that girdles the tepeguaje tree for the sole purpose of completing its life cycle by ovipositing eggs into the fallen branches.

Afraid of spiders? Many arachnids reside in our four-county area and one of the most commonly seen in the wild is the Texas Tan Tarantula. Although a mighty hunter, it is quite docile and friendly, feasting on flies, mosquitoes, cockroaches and crickets. Why would you ever need bug spray if you have the Texas Tan around?

As we know more about these and other wonderful insects, the task of preserving our land and its living marvels takes on excitement and urgency.

Carrie Cate
Alamo, Texas

Carrie Cate is an accomplished entomologist, teacher and interpretive naturalist. She is also involved in many projects in the Rio Grande Valley to restore native vegetation for wildlife habitat.

101

BUTTERFLIES and MOTHS

Black Swallowtail Caterpillar
For several weeks the dill plants were full of Black Swallowtail Caterpillars. We thought we had time to photograph them. However, we forgot just what a scrumptious meal the little fellows were to birds. It took us quite a long time to find this beauty.

First Place
(Fifth Place: Insects and Arachnids Division)
Photographer: Joseph Holman and Wallace Prukop
Landowner: Wallace Prukop

Canon EOS 1 with Canon 28-105mm f/4.5 lens; Kodachrome 64

Dusky-blue Groundstreak

An early spring rain caused many of the subtropical trees and shrubs to burst into bloom, and a pretty little groundstreak butterfly found the flowers of mesquite particularly attractive, sipping nectar as it posed for its portrait.

Second Place

Photographer: John and Gloria Tveten
Landowner: Rosemary and Cleve Breedlove –
The Inn at Chachalaca Bend

Minolta X-700 with Minolta 50mm macro lens and Sunpack ringlight; f/16 @ 1/60 sec.; Fuji Velvia

Sphingicampa Caterpillar

A showy, silver-spined caterpillar of a Sphingicampa moth was one of the most beautiful we had ever seen. Here it feeds voraciously on the foliage of a huisache tree.

Third Place

Photographer: John and Gloria Tveten
Landowner: Rosemary and Cleve Breedlove –
The Inn at Chachalaca Bend

Minolta X-700 with Minolta 50mm macro lens and Sunpack ringlight; f/16 @ 1/60 sec.; Fuji Velvia

ARACHNIDS

Tarantula
It was really hard during the drought we had last year to find things to photograph. Thankfully, we had a few days of light rain, which was enough to make the tarantulas come out to be photographed.
First Place
Photographer: Joseph Holman and Wallace Prukop
Landowner: Wallace Prukop

Canon EOS 1 with Canon 28-105mm f/4.5 lens;
f/4.5 @ 1/125 sec.; Kodachrome 64

Tarantula

Finding a caliche pit on an overcast day, I decided to return when there were some clouds and blue sky. I got down low and shot upward to get this effect.

Second Place

Photographer: Derrick Hamrick and Robert E. Summers
Landowner: Jim and Kathy Collins and Carolyn Cook Landrum –
Cook Ranch Properties

*Canon EOS 3 with Canon 24mm 3.5 tilt/shift lens;
f/11 @ 1/200 sec. with fill flash; Fuji Sensia 100*

Wolf Spider

I took many photos of arachnids during the photo contest. A Wolf Spider with a cricket posed long enough for me to shoot two or three rolls of film.

Third Place

Photographer: Bill Draker and Glenn Hayes
Landowner: Dr. Gary M. Schwarz, Dr. Steve Shepard and Partners –
Tecomate Ranch

*Canon EOS 3 with Canon 180mm macro lens and
550 EX flash; f/16 @ 1/180 sec.; Fuji Sensia 100*

BEES, WASPS and KIN

‹ **Paper Wasp**
One can only spend so many hours in a blind. I got out to stretch and noticed Paper Wasps stopping at my little water hole to drink. Grabbing my macro set-up, I lay down at the edge of the pond to photograph the wasps, not noticing the fly until I looked at the slide under magnification.

First Place
(Fourth Place: Insects and Arachnids Division)
Photographer: David Welling
Landowner: Pérez Ranch – Rancho San Francisco

Nikon F5S with Nikon F5 300mm f/3.5-4.5 AF lens with 6T close up diopter; f/11 @ 1/125 sec. with fill flash - SB28; Fuji Velvia pushed one stop

Paper Wasp
As the wasp crawled around the flower, I waited until I had a profile view and made sure the large compound eye was in focus. Use of flash ensured that the wasp's motion would be frozen on film.

Third Place
Photographer: Ralph Paonessa
Landowner: Joe Michael Castellano – Castellano Ranch

Canon EOS 3 with Canon EF 180mm f/3.5L macro lens; f/11 @ 1/200 sec. with two Canon 500 EX flashes; Fuji Velvia

Myrmicine Ant
Ants are always busy, and this one was certainly no exception. I used up two rolls of film to get this shot! The strong diagonal and tight curl of the plant give balance to the composition.

Second Place
Photographer: James Murray
Landowner: Camp Lula Sams

Canon EOS 1N with Canon 100mm f/2.8 macro lens, EF2x teleconverter and 25mm tube; f11 @ 1/60 sec. with 3 Novatron Studio flash heads; Kodak E100VS

DRAGONFLIES and DAMSELFLIES

⟨ Eastern Amberwing
A patch of Common Sunflowers beside a quiet, sedge-lined pond harbored a number of dragonfly species. The bank of the flower head provided good texture and color contrast for framing a perching Eastern Amberwing.
First Place
(First Place: Insects and Arachnids Division)
Photographer: John and Gloria Tveten
Landowner: Rosemary and Cleve Breedlove – The Inn at Chachalaca Bend

Minolta X-700 with Minolta 100mm macro lens and Sunpack ringlight; f/11 @ 1/60 sec.; Fuji Velvia

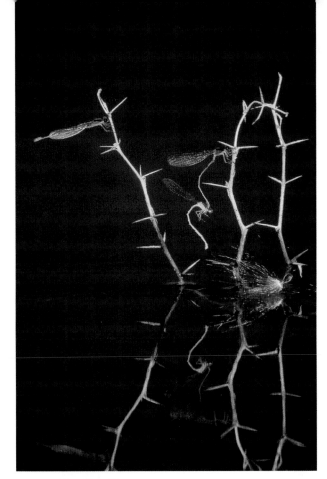

Blue-ringed Dancer
Freshly emerged from the quiet waters of a nearby pond, a Blue-ringed Dancer allowed us to approach closely as it clung to the stalk.
Second Place
Photographer: John and Gloria Tveten
Landowner: Rosemary and Cleve Breedlove – The Inn at Chachalaca Bend

Minolta X-700 with Minolta 50mm macro lens and Sunpack ringlight; f/16 @ 1/60 sec.; Fuji Velvia

Familiar Bluet
Sitting in my blind waiting for birds, I was drawn to the graphic of the dead twig with the seedpod. I repositioned myself to capture the graphic image just as the damselflies landed. Serendipity!
Third Place
Photographer: David Welling
Landowner: Pérez Ranch – Rancho San Francisco

Nikon F5S with Nikon 500 f/4 AF-S lens and TC-2DE 2x AF teleconverter; f/8 @ 1/250 sec.; Fuji Velvia pushed one stop

BEETLES

Blister Beetle

I was fascinated by the markings on the insect, and the ability of the macro lens to reveal details, such as the complex "mouth" structure and segmented legs.

First Place
(Second Place: Insects and Arachnids Division)
Photographer: Ralph Paonessa
Landowner: Joe Michael Castellano – Castellano Ranch

Canon EOS 3 with Canon EF 180mm f/3.5L macro lens; f/22 @ 1/200 sec. with two Canon 550EX flashes; Fuji Velvia

Dung Beetle

We had searched systematically for the colorful Scarab Beetles with no success. Finally one evening as we negotiated one of the rougher spots on the road, a beautiful little fellow flew onto the hood of the truck. Searching for ways to photograph him and still retain the character of the surroundings, I shot from a low angle, which permitted a background that was a complete reflection of the sky and trees to one side.

Second Place

Photographer: John D. and Adrienne Ingram
Landowner: Bentsen Palm Development

Nikon F5 with Nikon 200mm macro lens;
f/22 @ 1/30 sec.; Fuji Provia

Long-horned Beetle

Some Long-horned Beetles in the family *Cerambycidae* rank among the largest and most colorful of all our many beetle species. Characterized by their long antennae, they frequently sport brightly iridescent hues.

Third Place

Photographer: Marilyn Moseley LaMantia and Brenda Moseley Holt
Landowner: Jack Scoggins Jr. – Starr Feedyards, Inc.

Canon EOS 10S with Canon EOS 100mm macro lens;
f/16 @ 1/60 sec.; Fuji Provia 400

ALL OTHER INSECTS

Green Stink Bug

Upon discovering a bright green bug on the flower head of a
Common Sunflower, we waited until it had climbed up high enough
to be isolated against the yellow ray flowers and balanced by the dark
central disk in the lower corner.

First Place
(Third Place: Insects and Arachnids Division)
Photographer: John and Gloria Tveten
Landowner: Rosemary and Cleve Breedlove –
The Inn at Chachalaca Bend

*Minolta X-700 with Minolta 50mm macro lens and
Sunpack ringlight; f/16 @ 1/60 sec.; Fuji Velvia*

Katydid
A green Katydid is well camouflaged among the grasses as it feeds on the tender vegetation. It relies on its leaf-like shape and color for protection from a host of hungry predators, including birds, mammals, lizards, spiders and even other insects.

Second Place
Photographer: Jim Goin
Landowner: Neal and Gayle Runnels – La Lantana Ranch

(no technical information provided)

Katydid
I found this beautiful insect on the window screen at night and placed it on a flower in my tabletop "studio." When it slowly crawled to face me, I knew I had a potentially winning shot.

Third Place
Photographer: Ralph Paonessa
Landowner: Joe Michael Castellano – Castellano Ranch

Canon EOS 3 with Canon EF 180mm f/3.5L macro lens; f/8 @ 1/200 sec. with two Canon 550EX flashes; Fuji Velvia

ALL OTHER ARTHROPODS and SNAILS

‹ Rabdotus Land Snail
After using several rolls of film to feature a Greater Roadrunner feasting on this little guy's companions, I rescued him, which provided a great subject.
First Place
Photographer: Michael Francis and Mark S. Werner
Landowner: McAllen Properties

Nikon F4 with Nikon 75-180mm macro lens;
f/11 @ 1/125 sec.; Fuji Sensia 100

Fiddler Crab *(Top Right)*
When Fiddler Crabs feel threatened, they often retreat to small holes in the ground. After heavy rains soaked the area, these crabs became active. Coyotes and raccoons, known opportunists, dine on the crabs they can catch.
Second Place
Photographer: Tom Urban
Landowner: King Ranch

Canon F1 with Canon FD 80-200mm f.4 macro lens;
f/4 @ 1/125 sec.; Kodak E100VS

Striped Centruroides Scorpion
In the category "All Other Arthropods and Snails," the scorpion is one of the most interesting. It is feared by most people and regarded as an enemy. It can inflict a sting that is very painful.
Third Place
Photographer: Bill Draker and Glenn Hayes
Landowner: Dr. Gary M. Schwarz, Dr. Steve Shepard and Partners – Tecomate Ranch

Canon EOS 3 with Canon 180mm macro lens and
550EX flash; f/16 @ 1/200 sec.; Kodak EBX100

FOURTH & FIFTH PLACE WINNERS

Red-rim Melania
After spending several weeks photographing fast-moving birds around a small pond, I turned my attention to the literally thousands of small snails that inhabited the pond. It was nice for a change not to have the subject move as I pressed the shutter button.

Fifth Place
Category: All Other Arthropods and Snails
Photographer: Randall Ennis
Landowner: Baldo Jr. and Daniel Vela – San Pedro Ranch

Canon A2E with Canon 70-200mm f/2.8L lens and Nikon close-up 6T filter; f/16 @ 1/60 sec.; Fuji Sensia 100

Paper Wasp
When the wasp crawled into a position parallel to the camera, I made the shot, which rendered almost the entire body in focus.

Fifth Place
Category: Bees, Wasps and Kin
Photographer: Ralph Paonessa
Landowner: Joe Michael Castellano – Castellano Ranch

Canon EOS 3 with Canon EF 180mm f/3.5L macro lens; f/11 @ 1/200 sec. with two Canon 550EX flashes; Fuji Velvia

Spreadwing Damselfly
The early morning rays of the sun found this damselfly still a little wet behind the ears. Because it was somewhat immobilized by the dew on its wings, I was able to get close enough for the shot.

Fifth Place
Category: Dragonflies and Damselflies
Photographer: Jim Goin
Landowner: Neal and Gayle Runnels – La Lantana Ranch

(no technical information provided)

Blister Beetle
Not only did a patch of Common Sunflowers prove attractive to a host of insect species, but the large flower heads provided a perfect background as beetles fed on the pollen and tender florets.

Fourth Place
Category: Beetles
Photographer: John and Gloria Tveten
Landowner: Rosemary and Cleve Breedlove – The Inn at Chachalaca Bend

Minolta X-700 with Minolta 50mm macro lens and Sunpack ringlight; f/16 @ 1/60 sec.; Fuji Velvia

Green Lynx Spider

I was inspecting the cacti around the ranch house when I saw this web and egg sac. When I looked closer, the spider suddenly appeared from behind the egg sac! It remained on the sac to protect it while I shot a roll of film.

Fourth Place
Category: Arachnids
Photographer: Windland Rice
Landowner: Dan and Tricia Drefke
– Skipper Ranch

Nikon N90S with Nikon 60mm macro lens; f/16 @ 1/125 sec.; Fuji Velvia

Bee Fly

On cloudy days or during the middle part of the day, I would spend hours beating the brush looking for insects to photograph with the macro lens and flash. This fly was one.

Fifth Place
Category: All Other Insects
Photographer: Bill Draker and Glenn Hayes
Landowner: Dr. Gary M. Schwarz, Dr. Steve Shepard and Partners –
Tecomate Ranch

Canon EOS 3 with Canon 180mm macro lens and 550EX flash; f/16 @ 1/200 sec.; Fuji Sensia

Striped Centruroides Scorpion and Spider

When I found a scorpion with its prey, I quickly got in as close as possible for an intimate look as it fed on its catch. It appeared to be watching me with one of its eyes.

Fourth Place
Category: All Other Arthropods and Snails
Photographer: Ralph Paonessa
Landowner: Joe Michael Castellano – Castellano Ranch

Canon EOS 3 with Canon TS-E 90mm f/2.8 tilt/shift lens, EF 2x teleconverter and EF25 extension tube; f/16 @ 1/200 sec. with two White Lightning studio strobes; Ektachrome E100VS pushed one stop

Forbes' Silkmoth

I found this moth outside around the porch light one night. From 11:00 that night to 9:00 the next morning I photographed the moth from various angles.

Fourth Place
Category: Butterflies and Moths
Photographer: Derrick Hamrick and Roberta E. Summers
Landowner: Jim and Kathy Collins and Carolyn Cook Landrum – Cook Ranch Properties

Canon EOS 3 with Canon 90mm f/2.8 tilt/shift lens; f/22 @ 1/200 sec. with flash; Fuji Sensia

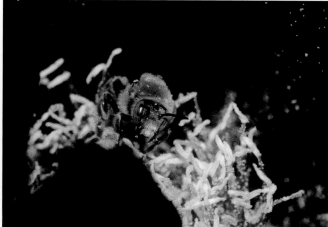

Bee

A beautiful bee, a Prickly Pear flower in full bloom, and proper full-flash exposure. Now why didn't I put the camera higher above that foreground petal and add a closeup lens to show the bee bigger?

Fourth Place
Category: Bees, Wasps and Kin
Photographer: Cliff Beittel
Landowner: Frank D. Yturria – Yturria Ranch

Canon EOS 3 with Canon 180mm f/3.5L lens and 2x teleconverter; f/22 @ 1/200 sec.; Fuji Provia F pushed one stop

Ceraunus Blue

The Valley enjoys a veritable bounty of butterflies each season that rivals birding in enjoyment by nature enthusiasts. It is hoped this wealth will continue, as The Valley Land Fund's message of the critical importance of habitat conservation spreads.

Fifth Place
Category: Butterflies and Moths
Photographer: James Murray
Landowner: Camp Lula Sams

Canon EOS 1N with Canon 100mm f/2.8 macro lens; f/16 @ 1/60 sec. with Novatron Studio flash heads; Kodak E100VS

Familiar Bluet

Here is a rather typical configuration of breeding damselflies. It was actually shot from some distance away using a moderately long lens. The only difficulty with such an image is getting perpendicular to the plane of the insects as they move around.

Fourth Place
Category: Dragonflies and Damselflies
Photographer: John D. and Adrienne Ingram
Landowner: Bentsen Palm Development

Canon EOS 1V with Canon 300mm f/4 IS lens and 2x teleconverter; f/11 @ 1/100 sec.; Fuji Provia

Long-horned Grasshopper
While photographing insects, I was interested to see a grasshopper moving cautiously across the Prickly Pear, using the flower pods as "stepping stones."

Fourth Place
Category: All Other Insects
Photographer: Sean Fitzgerald and Jeremy Woodhouse
Landowner: Roberto and Fran Yzaguirre

Canon EOS 3 with Canon EF 100 f/2.8 macro lens; f/11 @ 1/125 sec.; Kodak E100VS

Jumping Spider
Learning to do full-flash photography of insects and spiders was one of my favorite things about the 2000 contest. This aggressive and beautiful Jumping Spider lived on a Prickly Pear by one of the ranch's busiest gates.

Fifth Place
Category: Arachnids
Photographer: Cliff Beittel
Landowner: Frank D. Yturria – Yturria Ranch

Canon EOS 3 with Canon 180 mm f/3.5 lens, 2x teleconverter and 500 D closeup lens; f/22 @ 1/60 sec.; Fuji Provia F pushed one stop

Ground Beetle
By the looks of the massive mandibles on this specimen, you might surmise that it is a voracious predator. You would be right! The fairly large, colorful beetle is a great predator of caterpillars and other potentially destructive insects.

Fifth Place
Category: Beetles
Photographer: Hugh Lieck
Landowner: David C. and Diane Garza – El Monte del Rancho Viejo

Canon EOS 3 with Canon MPE 65 macro lens and Canon ringlight; f/16 @ 1/180 sec.; Fuji RVP

Hugh Lieck/David C. and Diane Garza

John and Gloria Tveten/Rosemary and Cleve Breedlove

Hugh Lieck/David C. and Diane Garza

Larry Ditto and Greg Lasley/Bud and Jimmy Payne

*Sean Fitzgerald and Jeremy Woodhouse/
Roberto and Fran Yzaguirre*

*Derrick Hamrick and Roberta E. Summers/
Jim and Kathy Collins and Carolyn Cook Landrum*

*Bill Draker and Glenn Hayes/
Dr. Gary M. Schwarz, Dr. Steve Shepard and Partners*

*Bill Draker and Glenn Hayes/
Dr. Gary M. Schwarz, Dr. Steve Shepard and Partners*

REPTILES AND AMPHIBIANS

Nothing in life is to be feared. It is only to be understood.

— Marie Curie

Robert L. Stanley/Carlos H. Cantu

My first encounter with a reptile occurred at about age six, when my brother brought a garter snake home in a coffee can from Boy Scout camp. Such a creature had never before been seen by me or my peers in our neatly trimmed suburb outside of Chicago, Illinois. I spent as many hours with that animal as I could; I remember allowing it to poke its slender head into places I could not see, like holes in the lamppost in our front yard. I thought it was very cool that the snake, with its ever-flickering red tongue, could go on adventures I would never be able to experience.

Eventually my mother, who did not share my enthusiasm for "wild things," ordered that our kinship be severed. Our neighbor claimed that a snake had once been seen in a nearby grassy field, and it was there my first snake friend was released.

My parents owned a series of nature books, and for years, they were my most significant contact with the real animal world. I studied pictures in the volume on dinosaurs, and I also pored repeatedly over the volume on reptiles. Of particular fascination to me were the egg-eating snake, and the geckos that voluntarily dropped their wiggling tails as decoys when accosted by predators.

Then, at nine years of age, I moved with my family to South Texas. I'll never forget my first night in our new house when I discovered a small light-colored lizard on my window screen. I whisked it into the house for a close inspection. At one point, it almost got away, and I grabbed its tail; it broke off and fell to the floor, dancing and wiggling. Just like in the books!

With a feeling of immense excitement, I realized that we had moved to the land they wrote books about!

I spent the next several years of my life exploring my urban neighborhood and enjoying the company of horned lizards, race runner lizards, spiny swifts, and of course, my legendary tail-dropping Mediterranean Geckos. But by the time I hit high school, their presence there was pretty much a thing of the past. Between home pesticides, Weed Eaters and wandering house cats, my neighborhood's herpetofauna was reduced to geckos and Gulf Coast Toads, two species that live much more easily by man's rules than the others.

I take my children out to visit my old buddies now, usually when we set out on camping trips in what few wild areas the Rio Grande Valley has left. There is satisfaction in knowing that organizations like The Valley Land Fund are working tirelessly to save a little habitat and help preserve some of our native plant and animal species.

The pages that follow are very special to me. These photos are like frozen magic moments from my earlier days, as well as reminders of some of my finest experiences as an adult. May their images touch your lives as they have mine.

Colette Adams
Brownsville, Texas

Colette Adams is the highly respected curator of reptiles at the Gladys Porter Zoo in Brownsville, Texas. She is well known for her educational programs on reptiles and amphibians.

TURTLES and TORTOISES

‹ Red-eared Turtle
Red-eared Turtles are common in many South Texas ponds. This fellow was crossing the road near a pond and showed his mood when I got too close.
First Place
(Third Place: Reptiles and Amphibians Division)
Photographer: Larry Ditto and Greg Lasley
Landowner: Bud and Jimmy Payne

Canon EOS 3 with Canon 180mm macro f/3.5L lens and 540 EZ flash; f/22 @ 1/90 sec.; Fuji Velvia pushed one stop

Red-eared Turtle
I can only guess at the nature of this meeting between two turtles. Most likely it was an overture to mating or a territorial standoff. After meeting nose to nose, one turtle tried to bite the other and a little pushing and shoving ensued. Eventually, the aggressor dropped off the log and swam away.
Third Place
Photographer: Irene Sacilotto
Landowner: Daniel Y. Butler – H. Yturria Land & Cattle

Nikon F5 with Nikon 600mm f/4 lens; f/5.6 @ 1/640 sec.; Kodak E100VS

Yellow Mud Turtle
The dragonfly was determined to sit on the mud turtle's nose. He returned time and time again. With the late evening light and the mirror reflection, it was hard to resist burning up some film.
Second Place
Photographer: Bill Draker and Glenn Hayes
Landowner: Dr. Gary M. Schwarz, Dr. Steve Shepard and Partners – Tecomate Ranch

Canon EOS 3 with Canon 400mm f/2.8 lens and 1.4x teleconverter; f/8 @ 1/500 sec.; Fuji Sensia 100

FROGS and TOADS

‹ Mexican Treefrog

I was quite delighted to spot this little critter sleeping on some exposed mesquite heartwood. I don't believe I'd seen one since my teens, and its big shiny eyes and enigmatic grin made it a very enticing subject.

First Place
(Fifth Place: Reptiles and Amphibians Division)
Photographer: Hugh Lieck
Landowner: David C. and Diane Garza – El Monte del Rancho Viejo

Canon EOS 3 with Canon EF 180mm f/3.5 macro lens and two Canon 550 EX flashes; f/22 @ 1/200 sec.; Fuji RVP

Marine Toad *(Top Right)*
I didn't expect to photograph toads. I was looking for some birds near a pond when I saw this couple jumping around.
Second Place
Photographer: David Melo
Landowner: Eddie and Alta Forshage – Cap Rock Pens

Canon EOS RT with Sigma AF 70-300mm DL lens and flash; f/5.6 @ 1/125 sec.; Fuji Sensia 100

Rio Grande Leopard Frog
I put my blind in a shallow pond near the frogs. It was like sitting in a cup of hot coffee. I inched up to the frogs for about 20 minutes and then photographed them with the camera barely above the water.
Third Place
Photographer: Sean Fitzgerald and Jeremy Woodhouse
Landowner: Roberto and Fran Yzaguirre

Canon EOS 1N-RS with Canon 300mm f/2.8 lens; Fuji Provia 100F

LIZARDS and SKINKS

Green Anole
Numerous palm trees at The Inn at Chachalaca Bend proved popular basking places for these lizards. One chose to pose alertly on a fresh corrugated frond.
First Place
(Fourth Place: Reptiles and Amphibians Division)
Photographer: John and Gloria Tveten
Landowner: Rosemary and Cleve Breedlove –
The Inn at Chachalaca Bend

Minolta X-700 with Minolta 50mm macro lens and Sunpack ringlight; f/11 @ 1/60 sec.; Fuji Velvia

Texas Horned Lizard
I took many shots to capture the "decisive moment" – just as the ant was about to become a meal.
Second Place
Photographer: Ralph Paonessa
Landowner: Joe Michael Castellano – Castellano Ranch

Canon EOS 3 with Canon TS-E 90mm f/2.8 tilt/shift lens and EF 1.4x teleconverter; f/16 @ 1/200 sec.; with two White Lightning studio strobes; Kodak E100VS pushed one stop

Green Anole
This Green Anole was about as subtle as a neon sign in Las Vegas every time he expanded his pink-colored pouch. But I guess the other lizards soon got the message – Stay away!
Third Place
Photographer: Stephen Sinclair
Landowner: Douglas Hardie

(no technical information provided)

NON-VENOMOUS SNAKES

Bullsnake
My first reaction any time I see a snake bigger than 18 or 20 inches is, "SNAAAKE!!!" It takes a few seconds for my brain to judge venomous or non-venomous, and remember that either way, there is a place for everything in nature.

First Place
Photographer: Hugh Lieck
Landowner: David C. and Diane Garza – El Monte del Rancho Viejo

Canon EOS 3 with Canon EF 180mm f/3.5 macro lens and two Canon 550 EX flash; Fuji RVP

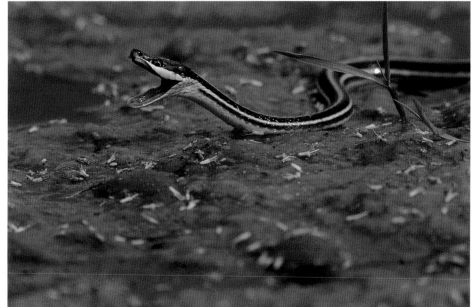

Western Ribbon Snake

The Western Ribbon Snake appears to be laughing, but it is actually resetting its jaw after swallowing an immature frog.

Second Place

Photographer: David Powell and Don Pederson
Landowner: Judge and Mrs. William Mallet – The Mary B. Ranch

Nikon F5 with Nikon 500mm f/4 AFS lens, Pk-13 extension tube and tripod; f/5.6 @ 1/250 sec.; Fuji Provia 100F

Western Ribbon Snake

A beautiful little snake allowed only infrequent glimpses as she routinely hunted for a meal among the lily pads. The light, the snake and the background eventually came together to portray the exquisite creature in her element.

Third Place

Photographer: Lynn Bieber-Weir and Ray Bieber
Landowner: Patric and Amy Ginsbach, Wayne and Chris Westphal – Palm Gardens, Inc.

Canon EOS 3 with Canon EF 500mm f/4 IS lens, 1.4x and 2x teleconverters, and 12.5 mm extension tube; f/11 @ 1/13 sec.; Kodak E100VS

VENOMOUS SNAKES

Western Diamondback Rattlesnake
Diamondback Rattlesnakes occasionally raise the forepart of the body above the ground to "smell" for prey and danger with their tongue. This profile shot shows such behavior while contrasting the subject against a background of green grass.
First Place
(Second Place: Reptiles and Amphibians Division)
Photographer: Larry Ditto and Greg Lasley
Landowner: Bud and Jimmy Payne

Canon EOS 1N with Canon 100-300mm AF lens;
f/5.6 @ 1/250 sec.; Fuji Velvia pushed one stop

Western Diamondback Rattlesnake

Searching for insects on a walk in the brush, I came across a rattler. Instead of fleeing, it began to "smell" me with its tongue. Lying low, I was able to take a couple of frames in the soft, diffused light.

Second Place

Photographer: Sean Fitzgerald and Jeremy Woodhouse
Landowner: Roberto and Fran Yzaguirre

Canon EOS 3 with Canon EF 100-400mm IS lens; f/5.6 @ 1/60 sec.; Kodak E100VS

Western Diamondback Rattlesnake

Rattlesnakes have always fascinated me, so it was a fun experience for me to spend so much time photographing this particular snake. Its posture with the rattle held high caught my eye.

Third Place

Photographer: Larry Ditto and Greg Lasley
Landowner: Bud and Jimmy Payne

Canon EOS 1N with Canon 180mm f/3.5L macro lens and 540 EZ flash used as fill; f/8 @ 1/125 sec.; Fuji Velvia pushed one stop

ALL OTHER REPTILES and AMPHIBIANS

‹ American Alligator

This ten-foot large male would have loved eating me, no kidding! My assistant hung bait 15 feet out over the water and above the camera view. When the alligator opened its mouth for a bite, I fired from the shallows.

First Place

(First Place: Reptiles and Amphibians Division; Best of Contest)

Photographer: Derrick Hamrick and Roberta E. Summers

Landowner: Jim and Kathy Collins and Carolyn Cook Landrum – Cook Ranch Properties

Canon EOS 3 with Canon 400mm f/2.8 IS lens; f/7.1 @ 1/250 sec.; Fuji Sensia 100

American Alligator *(Top Right)*

I constructed a small float, mounted my camera and remote control and pushed it towards the large gator via a long handle. On one occasion, after looking away for a second, it bit down on my float.

Second Place

Photographer: Derrick Hamrick and Roberta E. Summers

Landowner: Jim and Kathy Collins and Carolyn Cook Landrum – Cook Ranch Properties

Canon EOS 3 with Canon 24mm f/3.5 tilt/shift lens; f/16 @ 1/30 sec.; Fuji Sensia 100

Texas Banded Gecko

Geckos are neat little creatures. Their eyes are very interesting to me. We found many of them under rocks and around old logs. Macro photography gives us all a chance to see them a little closer.

Third Place

Photographer: Bill Draker and Glenn Hayes

Landowner: Dr. Gary M. Schwarz, Dr. Steve Shepard and Partners – Tecomate Ranch

Canon EOS 3 with Canon 180mm macro and 550 EX flash; f/16 @ 1/80 sec.; Fuji Sensia 100

FOURTH & FIFTH PLACE WINNERS

Texas Tortoise
Now, this is more my speed, a fun subject but stubborn as a mule. However, a long telephoto lens and 1.4x teleconverter (for increased magnification and working distance) were the neutralizer for its stubbornness to come toward the camera.

Fourth Place
Category: Turtles and Tortoises
Photographer: Kermit Denver Laird
Landowner: Juanita Farley – Speer Ranch

Nikon F5 with Nikkor 600mm f/4 AF-S lens and TC-14E 1.4x teleconverter; f/5.6 @ 1/250 sec.; Fuji Velvia @ ISO 40

Marine Toad
The toad jumped through an infrared beam, which triggered my camera and four high-speed flashes.

Fourth Place
Category: Frogs and Toads
Photographer: Derrick Hamrick and Roberta E. Summers
Landowner: Jim and Kathy Collins and Carolyn Cook Landrum – Cook Ranch Properties

Canon EOS 1N-RS with Canon 90 f/2.8 tilt/shift lens; f/16 @ 1/250 sec. with high speed flash; Fuji Sensia 100

Red-eared Turtle
Colorfully marked Red-eared Turtles are very shy. After I had encountered this one, its head and legs disappeared into its shell. Five minutes later the head emerged to give a good look to determine if I was still about.

Fifth Place
Category: Turtles and Tortoises
Photographer: Tom Urban
Landowner: King Ranch

Canon F1 with Canon 80-200mm f/4 macro lens; f/4 @ 1/30 sec.; Kodak E100VS

Texas Spotted Whiptail

This fast-moving terrestrial lizard is most active on warm sunny days. Usually located in dry, sparsely vegetated area, it spends most of its time snapping up tiny insects and interacting with other whiptails.

Fourth Place

Category: Lizards and Skinks
Photographer: Bill Plunkett and Bill Carter
Landowner: C.M. Cozad Ranch

Nikon F5 with Nikon AF 200mm macro lens; f/22 @ 1/250 sec.; Fuji Velvia

Gulf Coast Toad

I spent many nights searching and listening for singing males. It was easy to find toads, but they just would not carry a tune. Eventually, they called and I was right with them belly to belly in the shallows

Fifth Place

Category: Frogs and Toads
Photographer: Derrick Hamrick and Roberta E. Summers
Landowner: Jim and Kathy Collins and Carolyn Cook Landrum – Cook Ranch Properties

Canon EOS 1N-RS with Canon 90 f/2.8 tilt/shift lens; f/11 @ 1/200 sec.; Fuji Sensia 100

Texas Horned Lizard

Characteristically spiky, like a South Texas cactus, the horned lizard needs sun, high temperatures and undisturbed habitat in order to thrive. As with any heat-loving reptile, it has a high metabolic rate and must consume volumes of small crawling insects, especially ants, in order to meet its energy requirements.

Fifth Place

Category: Lizards and Skinks
Photographer: Robert L. Stanley
Landowner: Carlos H. Cantu – Cantu Ranch

Nikon N8008 with Nikon 55mm macro lens; f/8 @ 1/60 sec.; Fuji Sensia 100

Great Plains Ratsnake
After being disturbed, the snake showed its displeasure by coming after the "disturber" a couple of times before crawling under the rock to resume its nap.
Fifth Place
Category: Non-venomous Snakes
Photographer: Lee Kline
Landowner: Jim and Kathy Collins and Carolyn Cook Landrum – Cook Ranch Properties

Canon EOS RT with Canon EOS EF 70-200mm f/2.8L lens and extension tube; fill-flashed; Fuji Velvia pushed one stop @ ISO 80

Bullsnake
The old term "bull of the woods" applied to this Bullsnake. They seem to be born with ornery dispositions. I recognized the snake's loud hissing and striking pose soon enough to stay beyond its reach.
Fourth Place
Category: Non-venomous Snakes
Photographer: Tom Urban
Landowner: King Ranch

Canon F1 with Canon FD 80-200mm f/4 macro lens; f/4 @ 1/125 sec.; Kodak E100VS

Western Diamondback Rattlesnake
One afternoon I arrived at El Desierto, a favorite area to photograph, and discovered Western Diamondback Rattlesnakes mating in the road. I felt fortunate because the snakes were situated where sand had blown across the road and covered tire tracks, leaving no visible signs of man in the picture.
Fourth Place
Category: Venomous Snakes
Photographer: Ruth Hoyt
Landowner: Guerra Brothers

Canon 1V-HS with Canon 100-400mm f/4.5-5.6 IS lens; f/11; Fuji Sensia 100

Western Diamondback Rattlesnake
The hardest part of making the picture was getting my nerve up, particularly for moving the intervening grass to the side to allow a clear view of the head of the snake.

Fifth Place
Category: Venomous Snakes
Photographer: Kermit Denver Laird
Landowner: Juanita Farley – Speer Ranch

Nikon F5 with Nikkor AF 200mm f/4 D micro lens; f/16 @ 1/8 sec.; Kodak E100VS

Mediterranean Gecko
Mediterranean Geckos are alien lizards that apparently reached the Texas coast on ships and spread widely throughout the region. Here, one is prowling at night among the fallen fronds of a palm tree.

Fourth Place
Category: All Other Reptiles and Amphibians
Photographer: John and Gloria Tveten
Landowner: Rosemary and Cleve Breedlove – The Inn at Chachalaca Bend

Minolta X-700 with Minolta 50mm macro lens and Sunpack ringlight; f/16 @ 1/60 sec.; Fuji Velvia

Texas Banded Gecko
There are many different species of geckos, several of which are found in the Rio Grande Valley. I discovered them to be very gentle animals and enjoyable to photograph.

Fifth Place
Category: All Other Reptiles and Amphibians
Photographer: Bill Draker and Glenn Hayes
Landowner: Dr. Gary M. Schwarz, Dr. Steve Shepard and Partners – Tecomate Ranch

Canon EOS 3 with Canon 180mm macro lens and 550 EX flash; f/16 @ 1/200 sec.; Fuji Sensia 100

Derrick Hamrick and Roberta E. Summers/
Jim and Kathy Collins and Carolyn Cook Landrum

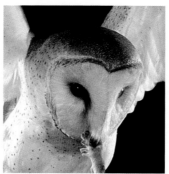

Kermit Denver Laird/Juanita Farley

Sean Fitzgerald and Jeremy Woodhouse/
Roberto and Fran Yzaguirre

Tom Urban/King Ranch

Ralph Paonessa/Joe Michael Castellano

John and Gloria Tveten/Rosemary and Cleve Breedlove

Sean Fitzgerald and Jeremy Woodhouse/
Roberto and Fran Yzaguirre

Bill Draker and Glenn Hayes/
Dr. Gary M. Schwarz, Dr. Steve Shepard and Partners

SPECIAL CATEGORIES

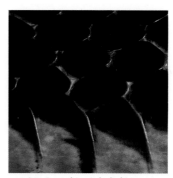

As long as I live, I'll hear waterfalls and birds and winds sing. I'll interpret the rocks, learn the language of flood, storm, and avalanche. I'll acquaint myself with the glaciers and wild gardens, and get as near the heart of the world as I can.

— John Muir

Larry Ditto and Greg Lasley/Bud & Jimmy Payne

La naturaleza viene del corazon de Dios pero nosotros la tenemos en nuestras manos. (Nature comes from God's heart but is held in our hands.)

Living ten years on a Starr County ranch in La Victoria changed my way of viewing life in the Rio Grande Valley forever. Those years were filled with wonder, struggles, discovery, adventure and learning to live in harmony with the creatures who shared our little piece of earth.

Drought, hurricanes, a tornado, spectacular sunrises and sunsets, double rainbows, intriguing cloud formations, dust storms, unrelenting and intense sunlight, bejeweled night skies and humid peaceful dawns were the backdrops of our existence on Farm Road 2360. Added to these were the sounds from the animal world: the howl of a Coyote, hoot of an owl, rustle of grass as a Javelina scurried along, the buzz of insects, the cry of a hawk overhead—all reminded us we were not alone.

Neighbors often gathered at our ranch in the evenings, under the mesquite trees that looked out over native brushlands, to share stories, keep up on local news, and to educate gently this northern gringa in the ways of ranch life. It is during these times that I learned to appreciate the richness and multidimensional aspects of South Texas wildlife. I learned of the influences of man, weather, natural events and behaviors that stimulated life and death in the animal world.

Here, in Special Categories, a single frame may capture that same integration of nature and its influences. Action, drama, humor and beauty unfold in the photographs, giving us unforgettable images of the diversity and complexities of life in the Rio Grande Valley.

To a lesser eye it would seem as if the land north of the river was simply a tangle of trees, grasses, stickers and brush with patches of barren prairie. To the anxious photographer it is a grand stage with an impending story that may unfold in a split second.

The added dimension to the photograph, suggested by the category, brings the viewer to an awareness of events and challenges these creatures experience. Not only do we appreciate the beauty of the animal but circumstances of a moment in its life. The skill and patience of these photographers are extraordinary. The results are to be treasured, for there may never be another moment quite like the ones you will see here.

My memories of La Victoria Ranch include clouds of butterflies floating around wildflowers, my baby asleep in the hammock between two mesquite trees with a Green Jay keeping watch, and a Western Diamondback Rattlesnake slithering along the path. Everything in delicate balance. Everything from God's heart now to our hands.

Joanna Rivera Stark
Desert Hot Springs, California

Educator, naturalist and writer Joanna Rivera Stark is the founder of the South Texas Chapter of the North American Butterfly Association. She is featured as Mother Nature at many festivals, educating children on the importance of conservation.

NIGHT PHOTOGRAPHY

‹ Barn Owl

Barn Owls were nesting in a deer blind. They would make a landing 15 feet above the ground on this post.

First Place
(Fifth Place: Special Categories Division)
Photographer: Derrick Hamrick and Roberta E. Summers
Landowner: Jim and Kathy Collins and Carolyn Cook Landrum – Cook Ranch Properties

Canon EOS 1N-RS with Canon 90mm f/2.8 tilt/shift lens; f/16 @ 1/250 sec. with high speed flash; Fuji Sensia 100

Striped Centruroides Scorpion *(Top Right)*

The most common scorpion found throughout Texas, Centruroides is nocturnal and found under rocks, logs and in human dwellings. Their sting is painful, though seldom deadly. For unknown reasons the hard chitinous exoskeleton glows under black (ultra-violet) light.

Second Place
Photographer: Brian and Shirley Loflin
Landowner: Robert J. Goodwin – Las Campanas Ranch

Nikon F5 with Nikon 105mm macro lens; f/5.6 @ 1/30 under black light; Fuji Provia 100F

Sphingicampa Moth

Although less well known, many of our moths prove as attractive as the more popular butterflies. This Sphingicampa, a member of the silkmoth family, was attracted to the lights at night and perched in an ebony tree beside our porch.

Third Place
Photographer: John and Gloria Tveten
Landowner: Rosemary and Cleve Breedlove – The Inn at Chachalaca Bend

Minolta X-700 with Minolta 50mm macro lens and Sunpack ringlight; f/16 @ 1/60 sec.; Fuji Velvia

ACTION

⟨ Javelina (Collared Peccary)
The sun was dying and the action just beginning when a herd of fourteen Javelinas wandered into the scene. Sibling rivalry? Javelinas are known to be aggressive. These two are certainly no exception.
First Place
(First Place: Special Categories Division)
Photographer: Kermit Denver Laird
Landowner: Juanita Farley – Speer Ranch

Nikon F5 with Nikkor 600mm f/4 AF-S lens and TC-14E 1.4x teleconverter; f/5.6 @ 1/30 sec.; Kodak Ektachrome E100VS

Bobcat *(Top Right)*
The picture was taken near the Bobcat's hiding place as it headed for cover.
Second Place
Photographer: Derrick Hamrick and Roberta E. Summers
Landowner: Jim and Kathy Collins and Carolyn Cook Landrum –
Cook Ranch Properties

Nikon F4 with Nikon 75-300mm f/5.6 zoom lens; f/5.6 @ 1/125 sec.; Fuji Velvia 50

Mallard
Prior to snapping the shot, I had detached my EOS 3 camera from the lens and placed it in a plastic container that stayed afloat inside my blind. After attaching the 1N-RS camera, I looked back to see my container and EOS 3 sinking beneath the surface.
Third Place
Photographer: Derrick Hamrick and Robert E. Summers
Landowner: Jim and Kathy Collins and Carolyn Cook Landrum –
Cook Ranch Properties

Canon EOS 1N-RS with Canon 400mm f/2.8 IS lens and 2x teleconverter; f/5.6 @ 1/500 sec.; Fuji Sensia 100

SPECIAL WILDLIFE SPECIES

‹ Northern Harrier
It had been a good morning for raptors – two Northern Harriers and a Red-tailed Hawk. The harrier, after some hesitation, came to the edge of the water hole and bathed. I was shooting at ground level from a blind in a hole in the ground.

First Place
Photographer: Sean Fitzgerald and Jeremy Woodhouse
Landowner: Roberto and Fran Yzaguirre

Canon EOS 3 with Canon EF 600m f/4 lens and 1.4x teleconverter; f/5.6 @ 1/350 sec.; Kodak E100VS

Northern Harrier
This Northern Harrier was one of three that I saw that day. It did not seem to be too disturbed by my presence, but rather curious, especially when I fired the shutter.

Third Place
Photographer: Sean Fitzgerald and Jeremy Woodhouse
Landowner: Roberto and Fran Yzaguirre

Canon EOS 3 with Canon EF 600mm f/4 lens; f/5.6 @ 1/500 sec.; Kodak E100VS

Common Snipe
Mirrored in a quiet pond, a snipe paraded back and forth as it probed in the mud for worms. Its eyes are placed far back on the sides of its head so that it can watch for danger as it feeds.

Second Place
Photographer: John and Gloria Tveten
Landowner: Rosemary and Cleve Breedlove – The Inn at Chachalaca Bend

Minolta X-700 with Novoflex 600mm lens and tripod; f/11 @ 1/250 sec.; Fuji Provia 100F

SUNRISE/SUNSET

‹ White-tailed Deer

A fine White-tailed buck stands alert in a crimson blood sunset. His commanding presence speaks to us that a wilderness still exists. Such a moment in time reduces distinctions between real life and dreams.

First Place
(Third Place: Special Categories Division)
Photographer: Tom Urban
Landowner: King Ranch

Canon F1 with Canon FD 400mm f/2.8L lens; f/2.8 @ 1/60 sec.; Fuji Velvia

Western Diamondback Rattlesnake

At sundown, I frantically pressed myself to the ground to get the snake framed against a tiny band of color in the sky. I ended up with dozens of stickers embedded in my knees and elbows, but I got the shot.

Second Place
Photographer: Sean Fitzgerald and Jeremy Woodhouse
Landowner: Roberto and Fran Yzaguirre

Canon EOS 1N-RS with Canon 70-200mm f/2.8 lens; f/5.6 @ 1/30 sec.; Kodak E100VS pushed one stop

Rio Grande Leopard Frog

Double exposures are somewhat easy. This frog with the setting sun is one. I photographed the sun and then waited for the dark. Then I used the same camera and a flash. I could do only one per day.

Third Place
Photographer: Bill Draker and Glenn Hayes
Landowner: Dr. Gary M. Schwarz, Dr. Steve Shepard and Partners – Tecomate Ranch

Canon EOS 3 with Canon 500mm f/4 IS lens (sun) and 180mm macro lens with 550 EX flash (frog); f/11 @ 1/125 (sun) and f/16 @ 1/200 sec. (frog); Fuji Sensia 100

MACRO PHOTOGRAPHY

‹ **Katydid**

I watched the insect awhile, and then was ready when it began drawing its legs through its mandibles as if to clean them.

First Place

(Second Place: Special Categories Division)

Photographer: Ralph Paonessa

Landowner: Joe Michael Castellano – Castellano Ranch

Canon EOS 3 with Canon EF 180mm f/3.5L macro lens; f/8 @ 1/200 sec. with two Canon 550EX flashes; Fuji Velvia

Long-horned Grasshopper

Macro photography gives us all a chance to see some of the little creatures of the world. This grasshopper was quite large, but seeing its face up close furnishes us with a new perspective.

Third Place

Photographer: Bill Draker and Glenn Hayes

Landowner: Dr. Gary M. Schwarz, Dr. Steve Shepard and Partners – Tecomate Ranch

Canon EOS 3 with Canon 180mm lens with 550 EX flash; f/16 @ 1/125 sec.; Fuji Sensia 100

Paper Wasp

I lay down at the edge of the pond and was rewarded with some great photos of some very cooperative wasps.

Second Place

Photographer: David Welling

Landowner: Pérez Ranch – Rancho San Francisco

Nikon F5S with Nikon 300mm f/3.5-5.6 AF lens with 6T close focus diopter; f/11 @ 1/125 sec.; Fuji Velvia pushed one stop

CAMOUFLAGE/ MIMICRY

Rustic Sphinx Moth
A piece of mesquite wood offered a fine camouflage
background for a moth.
First Place
(Fourth Place: Special Categories Division)
Photographer: Derrick Hamrick and Roberta E. Summers
Landowner: Jim and Kathy Collins and Carolyn Cook Landrum –
Cook Ranch Properties

Canon EOS 1N-RS with Canon 90mm f/2.8 tilt/shift lens;
f/22 @ 1/4 sec.; Fuji Sensia 100

Eastern Screech-Owl

I walked by a dead stump the previous morning and a screech owl flew out of it, almost knocking me over. The next morning, I stared at the stump for 20 minutes before I finally saw the owl blink. I have never seen such a beautiful camouflage job by a bird before.

Second Place
Photographer: David Welling
Landowner: Pérez Ranch – Rancho San Francisco

Nikon F5S with Nikon 500mm f/4-AF-S lens; f5.6 @ 1/125 sec.; Fuji Velvia pushed one stop

Western Diamondback Rattlesnake

In South Texas I often hear the warning, "Watch out for the rattlesnakes." Well, most nature photographers hope to cross trails with a large rattler. I lucked out to find this beautiful rattlesnake basking in the afternoon rays.

Third Place
Photographer: Tom Urban
Landowner: King Ranch

Canon F1 with Canon FD 20-35mm f/3.5L lens; f/5.6 @ 1/60 sec.; Kodak E100VS

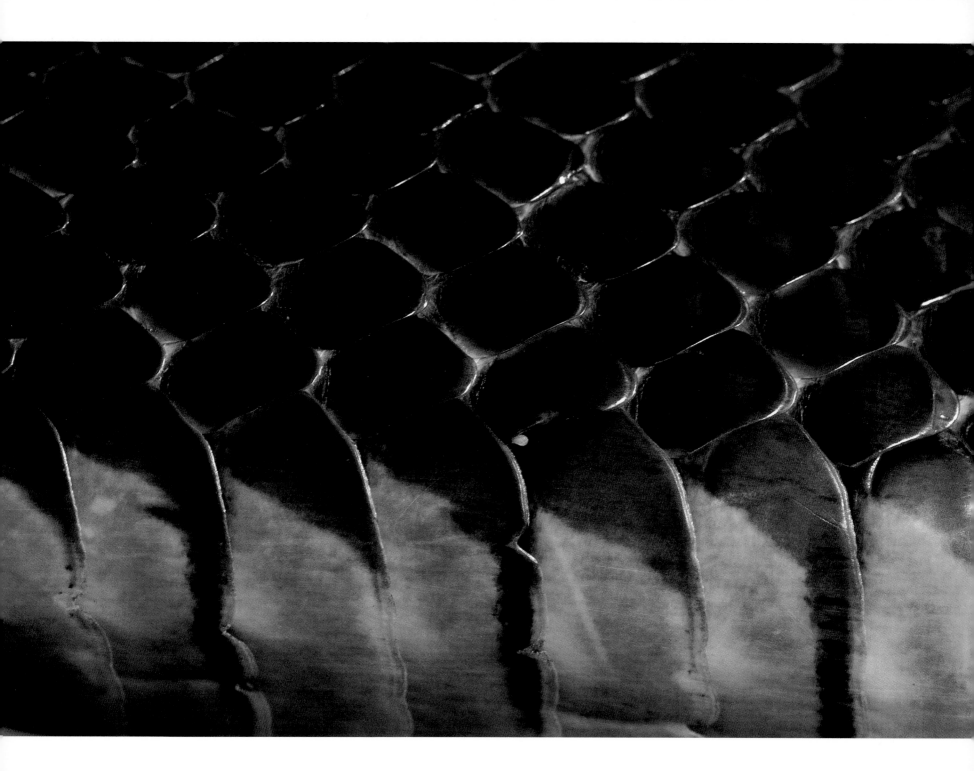

PATTERNS IN NATURE

< Texas Indigo Snake

I took a number of photos of this Texas Indigo Snake, but my wife convinced me to take a few shots of the beautiful scale pattern. I did not notice the tiny white parasite until I looked at the slides.

First Place
Photographer: Larry Ditto and Greg Lasley
Landowner: Bud and Jimmy Payne

Canon EOS 3 with Canon 180mm f/3.5L macro lens; f/8 @ 1/125 sec.; Fuji Velvia pushed one stop

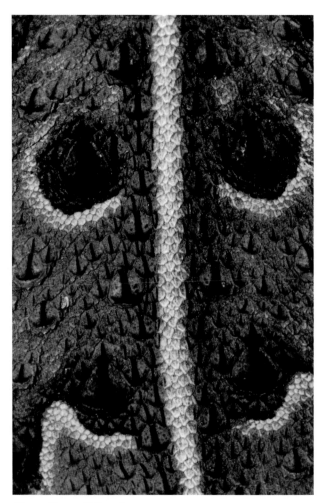

Tussock Moth

Attracted to our porch lights at night, a Tussock Moth, *Halysidota schausi*, had an intricate pattern that seemed to complement nicely the corrugated ribs of the palm frond on which it chose to perch.

Second Place
Photographer: John and Gloria Tveten
Landowner: Rosemary and Cleve Breedlove – The Inn at Chachalaca Bend

Minolta X-700 with Minolta 50mm macro lens and Sunpack ringlight; f/16 @ 1/60 sec.; Fuji Velvia

Texas Horned Lizard

I'm always on the lookout for unique patterns in the subjects I'm photographing. The back of the Texas Horned Lizard proved to be very interesting. This species is one of our more cooperative subjects to photograph in the South Texas brush.

Third Place
Photographer: Randall Ennis
Landowner: Baldo Jr. and Daniel Vela – San Pedro Ranch

Canon A2E with Canon 180mm f/3.5L lens and 540 EZ flash; f/16 @ 1/125 sec.; Fuji Sensia 100

Argiope Spider
Double exposure and a macro lens allowed me to compose an unusual image.
Fifth Place
Category: Night Photography
Photographer: Bill Draker and Glenn Hayes
Landowner: Dr. Gary M. Schwarz, Dr. Steve Shepard and Partners – Tecomate Ranch

Canon EOS 3 with Canon 500mm f/4 IS lens (moon) and 180mm macro lens with 550 EX flash (spider); f/11 @ 1/125 sec. (moon) and f/16 @ 1/125 sec. (spider); Fuji Sensia 100

Summer Tanager
It is hard not to notice a bright yellow Summer Tanager even concealed in foliage. Also, their robin-like song can be easily detected. This colorful female was perching near a popular watering hole waiting her turn to quench her thirst.
Fifth Place
Category: Special Wildlife Species
Photographer: Tom Urban
Landowner: King Ranch

Canon F1 with Canon FD 400mm f/2.8L lens and 1.4x-A teleconverter; f/4 @ 1/125 sec.; Fuji Velvia

White-tailed Deer
Being familiar with the habits of deer helped me capture this image. Some deer have tolerated my presence and do not perceive me as a threat. Over time, plus some luck, I managed to catch one in a sunset.
Fourth Place
Category: Sunrise / Sunset
Photographer: Tom Urban
Landowner: King Ranch

Canon F1 with Canon FD 400mm f/2.8L lens; f/8 @ 1/250 sec.; Fuji Velvia

Praying Mantis
A Praying Mantis poses on a flower across from the ranch house where we were staying.
Fifth Place
Category: Macro Photography
Photographer: Michael Francis and Mark S. Werner
Landowner: McAllen Properties

Nikon F4 with Nikon 75 - 180 macro lens; f/16 @ 1/125 sec.; Fuji Sensia 100

Rio Grande Leopard Frog

This fellow had come up on a small log to advertise for a mate.

Fourth Place
Category: Night Photography
Photographer: Larry Ditto and Greg Lasley
Landowner: Bud and Jimmy Payne

Canon EOS 3 with Canon 300mm EF f/2.8L lens, 2x teleconverter and 540 EZ flash; f/8 @ 1/90 sec.; Fuji Velvia pushed one stop

Harris's Hawk

The windmill, a favorite resting place for the Harris's Hawk, conveyed well a sense of place for the composition.

Fifth Place
Category: Sunrise / Sunset
Photographer: David Welling
Landowner: Pérez Ranch – Rancho San Francisco

Nikon F5S with Nikon 500mm f/4-AF-S lens and window mount; f/5.6 @ 1/1000; Fuji Velvia pushed one stop

Buff-bellied Hummingbird

Hummingbird photography requires lots of preparation, plenty of patience – and luck! I tried to capture the bird as he flew to the feeder, and here is the result. Multiple high-speed flash freezes the outspread wings.

Fourth Place
Category: Action
Photographer: Ralph Paonessa
Landowner: Joe Michael Castellano – Castellano Ranch

Canon EOS 3 with Canon EF 70 - 200mm f/2.8 L lens and EF 1.4x teleconverter; f/22 @ 1/200 sec.; with multiple flash @ 1/20,000 sec.; Fuji Velvia

Texas Tortoise

It seems we're all judged by speed in today's world – faster is better. Mahatma Gandhi said, "There is more to life than increasing its speed." I imagine the tortoise would agree.

Fifth Place
Category: Action
Photographer: Kermit Denver Laird
Landowner: Juanita Farley – Speer Ranch

Nikon F5 with Nikkor 600mm f/4 AF-S lens and TC-14E 1.4x teleconverter; f5.6@1/250 sec.; Fuji Velvia @ISO 40

Least Bittern
The smallest of herons, the Least Bittern can be difficult to find in South Texas marshes because of its perfect coloration.
Fourth Place
Category: Special Wildlife Species
Photographer: Hugh Lieck
Landowner: David C. and Diane Garza –
El Monte del Rancho Viejo

(no technical information provided)

Phaon Crescent
Awash in color from the surrounding blossoms, this little fellow stops long enough to allow me to focus carefully on its face. I find getting down to eye level one of the most enjoyable parts of the contest.
Fourth Place
Category: Macro Photography
Photographer: James Murray
Landowner: Camp Lula Sams

Canon EOS 1N with Canon 100mm f/2.8 macros lens, EF2x teleconverter and 25mm tube; f/16 @ 1/60 sec.; with 3 Novatron studio flash heads; Kodak E100VS

Short-horned Grasshopper
I was hiking down a trail during the last week of the contest, when I spotted this grasshopper. I was very lucky to see it because it matched its surroundings so well.
Fourth Place
Category: Camouflage/Mimicry
Photographer: Rex Hewitt
Landowner: J.D. Hensz – Rio Viejo

Canon EOS 1N with Canon 100mm f/2.8 macro lens; f/16 @ 1/125; Fuji Velvia

Sphingicampa Moth

Heavy overcast skies and strong winds had me sulking around camp. The moth was hanging on the protective screen of a bug zapper — one inch either way and poof, no picture! I coaxed the moth onto a stick and moved it to the fence for the shot.

Fifth Place
Category: Camouflage/Mimicry
Photographer: Lee Kline
Landowner: Jim and Kathy Collins and Carolyn Cook Landrum — Cook Ranch Properties

Canon EOS-RT with Canon EF 100mm f/2.8 lens with fill flash; Fuji Provia F @ ISO 100

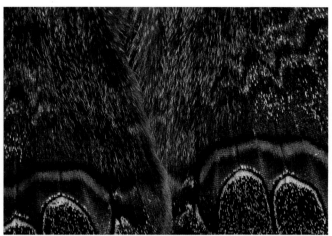

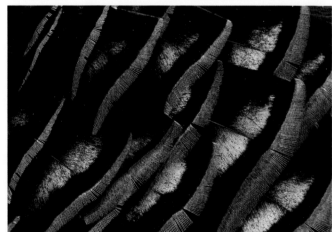

Black Witch Moth

If you look closely, carefully, you can find beauty everywhere in nature. At first glance, Black Witch Moths are just big brown bat-like moths. Close examination reveals these feathery hairs and iridescent scales.

Fourth Place
Category: Patterns In Nature
Photographer: Hugh Lieck
Landowner: David C. and Diane Garza – El Monte del Rancho Viejo

Canon EOS 3 with Canon 180mm f/3.5 marco lens and two 550 EX flashes; f/22 @ 1/200 sec.

Wild Turkey

One of the challenges in nature photography is making order out of chaos, and whether I'm photographing landscapes or a bird in flight, line, form and design intrigue me. I found all the elements, including texture, in these turkey feathers.

Fifth Place
Category: Patterns In Nature
Photographer: Larry Dech
Landowner: G & M Glick Ranch

Nikon F5 with Nikon 200mm micro lens; f/16 @ 1/15 sec.; Fuji Velvia

Left to Right:
Stephen Freligh,
Wyman Meinzer,
Darrell Gulin
Photo by
Audrey G. Martin

PHOTO CONTEST JUDGES

Steve Freligh

Formerly Director of Photography at the National Wildlife Federation, Steve Freligh is the founder and publisher of the award-winning *Nature's Best* magazine and director of the Nature's Best Foundation. Twenty years of publishing experience include consulting projects with Discovery Communications, Eastman Kodak Company, National Geographic Society and more. Freligh is the creator of the Nature's Best and Cemex International Photography Awards held annually at the Smithsonian National Museum of Natural History in Washington, D.C.

Wyman Meinzer

Wyman Meinzer's interests in outdoor photography began in 1974 after he received a degree in Wildlife Management from Texas Tech University. Since that time his images have appeared in over 300 magazines worldwide including *Smithsonian, Natural History, National Geographic, Time* and *Newsweek*. Meinzer has authored or photographed eleven major coffee table books on the natural and historical heritage of Texas. In 1993, he received the San Antonio Conservation Award for his book *Roadrunner,* and in 1997, he was designated "State Photographer of Texas" by the 75th Legislature.

Darrell Gulin

Based in the Seattle, Washington area, Darrell Gulin has been a professional nature photographer for the last 16 years. His work has been used by almost every major nature calendar line, including Audubon, Sierra Club, Kodak and Inner Reflections. Gulin has published credits with *Outdoor Photographer, Newsweek, National Geographic, National Wildlife, Audubon,* and *Popular Photography* magazines.

Gulin shares his knowledge in speaking engagements around North America and photography workshops through such entities as International Wildlife Adventures, Popular Photography mentor series, and Great American Workshops.

PROUD SPONSORS OF THE

fourth grade

NATURE PHOTO CONTEST

Shown here at the awards ceremony is Master of Ceremonies Richard Moore with 2001 First Grand Prize winner Hunter Cofoid and 2001 Second Grand Prize winner Marissa Shinsky. *Photo by Alvie Britton*

During the Fourth Grade Nature Photo Contest, children explored the natural areas of the Rio Grande Valley by photographing and documenting our native wildlife and its habitat. The contest is an excellent way for students to learn about the natural world while having fun.

2000 CONTEST
Chair: Marian DellaMaggiora

Contest Partners
TEAM 4 KGBT-TV
Rio Grande Birding Festival
Harlingen Area Chamber of Commerce

Bronze Medal Sponsors
Britton's Photo & Imaging
Grand Oak Junction
McDonald's
Region One Education Service
Treviño's Photo
Trophies Etc.

2001 CONTEST
Chair: Amy Johnson

Contest Partners
The University of Texas at
Brownsville
and Texas Southmost College
TEAM 4 KGBT-TV
McAllen International Museum

Gold Medal Sponsor
Target

Silver Medal Sponsors
Charles Clark Chevrolet
Texas Commission on the Arts
Weyerhaeuser

Bronze Medal Sponsors
Hales, Bradford & Allen, LLP, CPA
H.E.B
Johnson Brothers Construction
Klein Galleries
Gary and Laura Klinck
McAllen National Bank
Star of Texas Energy Services

Friends
David O. Adame, D.D.S.
Don Breeden and Pat Burchfield
Alvie Britton
DeLuna, Inc.
John A. Gerling, D.D.S.
Dr. Gene Grove
C. Wesley and Jane B. Kittleman
McDonald's

THE FOURTH GRADE NATURE PHOTO CONTEST

Taylor Kittleman / St. John's Episcopal School

If you wish your children to think deep thoughts, to know the holiest emotions, take them to the woods and hills, and give them the Freedom of the meadows; the hills purify those who walk upon them.

— Richard Jefferies

I have had the pleasure of being involved with The Valley Land Fund Fourth Grade Nature Photo Contest since its inception, and I believe it is a wonderful way of introducing children to the natural world around them. The great thing about nature photography is that it compels you to pause and acknowledge your environment, and that can easily lead to wonder, appreciation and respect.

When I was a fourth grade student at Travis Elementary in Harlingen, we studied about lions, tigers and polar bears, but little notice was given to our own South Texas wildlife. Perhaps we were still too busy conquering the remaining brushland in the late fifties to appreciate the denizens of the chaparral.

Fortunately, I lived adjacent to the Arroyo Colorado and spent my free time exploring the brush along the banks. Those childhood adventures were the basis for my love of nature. I now make my living photographing and writing about wildlife, but that sense of childhood wonder continues to accompany me on my treks.

Exposing children at an early age to the great outdoors is the best way to help ensure that they will mature into stewards of the land, and the fourth grade photo contest provides that positive exposure. The students have a great time photographing everything from neighborhood flocks of Red-crowned Parrots to lumbering Texas Tortoises, and the teachers love the opportunity for hands-on learning.

I cannot wait to see the excited faces of the hundreds of students at the next fourth grade photo awards ceremony. The folks at The Valley Land Fund can be assured that they are making a real difference for South Texas wildlife. Who knows, the next nature reporter for KGBT-TV just might be one of those aspiring young photographers who got their start with the help of The Valley Land Fund Fourth Grade Nature Photo Contest!

Richard Moore
San Benito, Texas

Richard Moore is a popular video photographer and environmentalist regularly featured on Valley television station KGBT-TV 4.

Horse Crippler Cactus
Photographer: Paola Garcia
School: Ringgold Elementary School, Rio Grande City

Inca Dove
Photographer: Jessica Taylor Rowland
School: Milam Elementary School, McAllen

Nine-banded Armadillo
Photographer: Jessica Taylor Rowland
School: Milam Elementary School, McAllen

Bird Nest
Photographer: Julianne Brittain
School: St. John's Episcopal School, McAllen

Box Turtle
Photographer: Stefano Palmieri
School: Martinez Elementary School, Sharyland

Ruby-throated Hummingbird
Photographer: Stacy Norcross
School: Episcopal Day School, Brownsville

164

Texas Tortoise
Photographer: Jennifer Trejo
School: Ringgold Elementary School, Rio Grande City

Dwarf Poinciana
Photographer: Taylor Kittleman
School: St. John's Episcopal School, McAllen

White-tailed Deer
Photographer: Nicholas Wilde
School: Episcopal Day School, Brownsville

Green Parakeets
Photographer: Gabriel Ochoa
School: Episcopal Day School, Brownsville

Walkingstick
Photographer: Matthew Rispoli
School: Episcopal Day School, Brownsville

Northern Mockingbird
Photographer: Leslie Ray
School: Episcopal Day School, Brownsville

Queen
Photographer: Ixchel Parr
School: St. John's Episcopal School, McAllen

Giant Swallowtail
Photographer: Hunter Cofoid
School: St. John's Episcopal School, McAllen

The Rio Grande River
Photographer: Nicholas Norris
School: St. John's Episcopal School, McAllen

Sunset Over The Laguna Madre
Photographer: Marissa Shinsky
School: St. Mary's Catholic School, Brownsville

Dolphins
Photographer: Brenda Reyna
School: El Jardin Elementary School, Brownsville

Brown Pelican
Photographer: Carolyn Urbis
School: Episcopal Day School, Brownsville

American Alligator
Photographer: Alexis Wells
School: St. Mary's Catholic School, Brownsville

Mourning Dove
Photographer: Elizabeth Wesley Kittleman
School: St. John's Episcopal School, McAllen

ACKNOWLEDGMENTS

Ixchel Parr/St. John's Episcopal School

For my part I consider the Earth very noble and admirable precisely because of the diverse alterations, changes, generations, etc., that occur in it incessantly.

— Galileo

PHOTO CONTEST SPONSORS

The Valley Land Fund would like to thank the corporate and individual sponsors who make the Wildlife Photo Contest and this book a possibility and a success. Through their commitment to the preservation of the Valley's unique natural treasures, and their vision in helping to create a new source of revenue for landowners, photographers and businesses, they are the heart and soul of this contest and have our unending gratitude.

Please visit these businesses and give them your support and heartfelt thanks. Tell them and other friends whose names you see here that you applaud their spirit and involvement.

We were proud to partner with The Nature Conservancy of Texas in the 2000 contest. The Nature Conservancy was attracted to the photo contest for its uniqueness among conservation events and the potential to raise significant funds to protect critical wildlife habitat that is at risk of being lost forever. This dynamic team brings the best of all elements together for wildlife. The Valley Land Fund is known for bringing new ideas to conservation and its steadfast loyalty to private landowners. The Nature Conservancy is the largest, oldest and most respected land trust in the nation.

Texas State Bank – 2000 Corporate Sponsor of the Year

The Valley Land Fund Wildlife Photo Contest named Texas State Bank as the 2000 Corporate Sponsor of the Year. Under the guidance of its CEO, Mr. Glen Roney, Texas State Bank became a sponsor of the very first Wildlife Photo Contest in 1994, and has been a sponsor for each contest since.

Mr. Roney and Texas State Bank exemplify the leadership, devotion, and constancy that will help to ensure the future prosperity of Valley wildlife. We thank them and all of our sponsors for making the Wildlife Photo Contest and this book possible.

PHOTO CONTEST SPONSORS

GRAND PRIZE
Wells Fargo

John and Audrey Martin

Loring Cook Foundation

JP Morgan Chase

Fuji Photo Film U.S.A., Inc.

B & H Photo

Clark Chevrolet

Bill and Susanne Robertson

Ruth A. Martin

Mildred Erhart in memory of Ted Erhart

Broadway Hardware

Team 4 KGBT TV

KURV710 TalkRadio

First Grand Prize
"The Vannie Cook Award" in memory of Vannie E. Cook Jr.

Texas State Bank

Boggus Motors

Valley Beverage, Inc. - Miller Lite

Second Grand Prize
Knapp Medical Center

A. Clayton Scribner

Third Grand Prize
"The Argyle & Margaret McAllen Award"
in memory of Argyle & Margaret McAllen

James A. McAllen Family

Magic Valley Electric Cooperative

Alamo Bank of Texas

Jones & Cook Stationers

Payne Dealer Group

Fourth Grand Prize
Bentsen Palm Development

Fifth Grand Prize
Central Power and Light

PHOTO CONTEST SPONSORS

DIVISION

Bill Burns

Children's Dental Center - Karen and Phil Hunke

Coastal Banc ssb

June and Carroll Elliott

Johnson Brothers Construction in memory of Britta Thompson

T.A. and Lucia Pollard

Shepard Walton King Insurance Group

Weyerhaeuser Company Foundation

Roger Zessin

CLASS

Aldrich, Smith & Baker

Anonymous

Russell and Jeannie Barron

Boultinghouse Simpson Architects

D. Wilson Construction Company

Fermata, Inc.

Frost National Bank

Guerra Brothers in honor of Rafael and Carmen Guerra

K & E Investment Company

Kittleman, Thomas, Ramirez & Gonzales PLLC

Chuck and Sandy Mann

Monte Lindo Ranch

Pete and Vicki Moore

Steve and Flora Parr

Schaleben Interests

Dr. Gary M. and Marlee Schwarz -Tecomate Ranch

Dr. Steve and Suzanne Shepard -Tecomate Ranch

Joan Tavarez

Robert Townsend

Valley Baptist Medical Center

OFFICIAL SPONSORS

Advantage Rent-a-Car

Britton's Photo & Imaging

Continental Airlines

McAllen Miller International Airport

ADDITIONAL SUPPORT

B104/KTEX

Russell Barron

Dr. Steve Bentsen

David Blankinship

Breeden, McCumber, Gonzalez Advertising and Design

Bill Burns

Alice G.K.K. East

Steve Freligh

Darrell Gulin

Inn at Chachalaca Bend

Amy and Kenneth Johnson

KRGV-TV Channel 5

Tom Koeneke

McAllen Nature Festival

Judy McClung

Wyman Meinzer

Virginia Meyer

Mission Butterfly Festival

Richard Moore

Bill Plunkett

Davis Rankin

Rhodes Farms Partnership

RGV Birding Festival

Santillana Ranch

Schaleben Interests

Smith, Fankhauser, Voigt & Watson PLLC

PHOTOGRAPHERS

Craig Abbott
Oklahoma City, OK

Ernesto Aguilar
Edinburg, TX

Leticia A. Alamia
St. Gabriel, LA

Charles L. Anderson
McAllen, TX

Paul Arant
Bessemer, AL

David Armstrong
Richmond, TX

Catalina Grace Bacod
Rio Grande City, TX

Kyle E. Barker
Austin, TX

Donald E. Bartram
Albuquerque, NM

Richard L. Beeckman
Saginaw, MI

Cliff Beittel
York, PA

Jim Benson
San Benito, TX

Steve Bentsen
McAllen, TX

Ray Bieber and Lynn Bieber-Weir
McAllen, TX

Jerry J. Box
McAllen, TX

Bill Burns
McAllen, TX

John Cancalosi
Slidell, LA

Bill Carter
Church Hill, TN

Bill Caskey
Austin, TX

Dwight and Dominique Chamberlain
Priest River, ID

Kathy Adams Clark
The Woodlands, TX

Tim Cooper
Rio Hondo, TX

Roscoe Creed
San Antonio, TX

Larry Dech
Grand Haven, MI

Michael Delesantro
Weslaco, TX

Vern Denman
McAllen, TX

Larry Ditto
McAllen, TX

Brad Doherty
Brownsville, TX

Jean Domansi
Rio Grande City, TX

Mary Donahue
Rio Hondo, TX

Bill Draker
San Antonio, TX

Carla Ellard
Edinburg, TX

John English
Laredo, TX

Randall Ennis
McAllen, TX

Dr. Lucile Estell
Rockdale, TX

Ted Falls Jr.
Alamo, TX

Robert J. Fisher
Port Aransas, TX

Sean Fitzgerald
Dallas, TX

Eddie and Alta Forshage
McAllen, TX

Michael Francis
Billings, MT

David Freshwater
Tucson, AZ

Omar Garcia
Austin, TX

Pete and Mary L. Garcia
Linn, TX

Diane Garza
Brownsville, TX

James Gift
Haslett, MI

Jim Goin
Fort Worth, TX

Gary Groves
McAllen, TX

Luciano E. Guerra
Mission, TX

Beto Gutierrez
Edinburg, TX

Derrick Hamrick
Raleigh, NC

Jay Hardy
Madisonville, TX

Betty Harris
Rockdale, TX

Jeffrey Hartman
Mesquite, TX

Glenn Hayes
Markham, TX

J. D. Hensz
Bayview, TX

Joe Hermosa
Brownsville, TX

Rex Hewitt
Laguna Vista, TX

Harold and Renee L. Hills
Lillian, TX

Joseph Holman
Brownsville, TX

Brenda Moseley Holt
Harlingen, TX

Ruth Hoyt
Spanish Lake, MO

Lowell Hudsonpillar
Mission, TX

John D. and Adrienne Ingram
Austin, TX

Mary Jo Janovsky
Rio Hondo, TX

Kenneth and Amy Johnson
McAllen, TX

Riesley and Carol Jones
McAllen, TX

Mike Kelly
Terrell, TX

Kathy Kilgore
Harlingen, TX

Lee Kline
Loveland, CO

Mike Krzywonski
Laguna Vista, TX

Fred LaBounty
Harker Heights, TX

Kermit Denver Laird
Starkville, MS

PHOTOGRAPHERS

Marilyn MoseleyLaMantia
Harlingen, TX

Greg Lasley
Austin, TX

J. Stephen Lay
Lacey, WA

Bill Leidner
Mission, TX

Hugh Lieck
Kingsville, TX

Brian and Shirley Loflin
Austin, TX

Dan Lyons
San Antonio, TX

David Manix
Rio Hondo, TX

Joel Martinez
Weslaco, TX

David Melo
Mission, TX

Donald Keith Montgomery
Lewisville, TX

Laura Elaine Moore
McAllen, TX

William Muñoz
Hamilton, MT

James Murray
Arlington, TX

Kathryn Neville
New Canaan, CT

Michael and Andrea Nisbet
Hotchkiss, CO

John P. O'Neill
St. Gabriel, LA

Ralph Paonessa
Ridgecrest, CA

Pete Parker
Port Aransas, TX

Richard Parker
Brownsville, TX

E. Weldon Parkhill
Edinburg, TX

Jim Pavlica
McAllen, TX

Rob Payne
Linn, TX

Jimmy Paz
Brownsville, TX

Don Pederson
Houston, TX

Jorge Pérez
McAllen, TX

Linda Peterson
Ventura, CA

Bill Plunkett
Longview, TX

David Powell
Houston, TX

Belinda Prude
Hebbronville, TX

Wallace Prukop
San Benito, TX

Maresa Pryor
Sarasota, FL

Donald S. Pye
Austin, TX

Roel Ramirez
Roma, TX

Caroline R. Reynolds
Hunt, TX

Windland Rice
Jackson, WY

Jim Rowland
McAllen, TX

Joe A. Roybal
Santa Fe, NM

Irene Hinke Sacilotto
Joppa, MD

Victor E. Sanchez
Edinburg, TX

Bill Scales
Burkeville, TX

John Schmid
McAllen, TX

Stephen Sinclair
Brownsville, TX

Brian Small
Los Angeles, CA

Robert L. Stanley
McCoy, TX

Jane Starling
Mission, TX

Lynn Starnes
Albuquerque, NM

Roberta E. Summers
Raleigh, NC

Ralph Thompson
Oklahoma City, OK

Ginger Tumlinson
Clute, TX

John L. and Gloria Tveten
Baytown, TX

Tom Urban
Falfurrias, TX

Kevin Vandivier
Lakeway, TX

Shannon Vandivier
Lakeway, TX

Ric Vasquez
Harlingen, TX

Tom Vezo
Green Valley, AZ

Carlos J. Villarreal
Brownsville, TX

Tony Vindell
Brownsville, TX

Leticia M. Volpe
Weslaco, TX

Sharon Waite
Mission, TX

Elizabeth P. Walker
Corpus Christi, TX

John Walters
San Antonio, TX

Jack Watson
Lake Charles, LA

David Welling
Canoga Park, CA

Mark S. Werner
Rock Falls, IL

Charlie West
Corpus Christi, TX

John Williams
Weslaco, TX

Jeremy Woodhouse
The Colony, TX

Paul G. Young
Weslaco, TX

Lee Zieger
Brownsville, TX

LANDOWNERS

The Valley Land Fund 2000 Wildlife Photo Contest included landowners in the following eight counties: Brooks, Cameron, Hidalgo, Jim Hogg, Kenedy, Starr, Willacy and Zapata.

Mary N. Baldridge
Starr

Calvin Bentsen
La Coma Ranch
Hidalgo

Bentsen Palm Development
Hidalgo

Rosemary and Cleve Breedlove
The Inn at Chachalaca Bend
Cameron

William Richard Buchholz
Starr

Bill Burns
Burns Ranch
Hidalgo

Daniel Y. Butler
H. Yturria Land and Cattle
Willacy

Camp Lula Sams
Cameron

Carlos H. Cantu
Cantu Ranch
Hidalgo

Joe Michael Castellano
Castellano Ranch
Hidalgo

Joe E. Chapa Family
San Manuel Farms
Hidalgo

Jonathan Cohrs
Cohrs Ranch
Hidalgo

Jim and Kathy Collins and
Carolyn Cook Landrum
Cook Ranch Properties
Hidalgo and Starr

Carl C. Conley
Conley Ranch
Willacy

C.M. Cozad Ranch
Hidalgo

Harry Cullen
Buena Vista Ranch
Cameron

Richard Drawe
Drawe Farms
Hidalgo

Dan and Tricia Drefke
Skipper Ranch
Brooks

Mary Donahue
Cameron

M.G. (Newt) and Maggie Dyer
Capote Farms, Inc.
Hidalgo

Ed Rachal Foundation
La Copa Ranch
Brooks

Juanita Farley
Speer Ranch
Starr

Mike Fitzpatrick
Cameron

Eddie and Alta Forshage
Cap Rock Pens
Hidalgo

Bert and Trudy Forthuber
Krenmueller Farms
Hidalgo

Marsha Gamel
Hidalgo

J.A. Jr. and Sue Ann Garcia
Garcia Ranch
Willacy

Dr. Martin and Celia Garcia
Hacienda La Esperanza
Willacy

David C. and Diane Garza
El Monte del Rancho Viejo
Cameron

Mark Gibbs
Rio Grande Container Game Ranch
Starr

Pat and Amy Ginsbach
Palm Gardens, Inc.
Hidalgo

G and M Glick Ranch
Brooks

Robert J. Goodwin
Las Campanas Ranch
Jim Hogg

Matt and Patty Gorges
Cameron

Guerra Brothers
Hidalgo and Starr

Douglas Hardie
Cameron

Virginia Lee Heath
Rancho Sacsayhuanman
Willacy

J.D. Hensz
Rio Viejo
Cameron

Shawn Horton
Rancho El Javalin
Hidalgo

Phil and Karen Hunke
El Tecolote Ranch
Hidalgo

Mary Jo Janovsky
RGV Shooting Center
Cameron

Kenneth and Amy Johnson
Hidalgo

Barbara L. Kennett
Cameron

King Ranch
Brooks and Kenedy

Robert J. Lerma
Palmito Ranch
Cameron

Judge and Mrs. William Mallet
The Mary B. Ranch
Willacy

LANDOWNERS

John and Audrey Martin
Hidalgo

Roy Martinez
2 M Ranch
Starr

James A. McAllen
McAllen Ranch Properties
Hidalgo

Margaret and Robert McAllen
Las Colmenas Ranch
Hidalgo

Charles and Christina Mild
Mild's on the Arroyo
Cameron

Monte Lindo Ranch
Hidalgo

The Nature Conservancy of Texas
Cameron and Hidalgo

Becky Parker
Phillips Ranch
Cameron

Bud and Jimmy Payne
Brooks

Jorge and Dilia Pérez
Santa Cecilia Ranch
Starr

Betty and Librada (Libby) Pérez
Pérez Ranch - Rancho San Francisco
Hidalgo

Billie C. Pickard
Pickard Partners
Willacy

Wallace Prukop
Cameron

Roel Ramirez
Starr

Rhodes Farms Plantation
Willacy

Bill Robertson
Minten Ranch
Brooks

Neal and Gayle Runnels
La Lantana Ranch
Willacy

Sabal Palm Audubon Sanctuary
Cameron

Emilio Sanchez
Cameron

Michael Scaief
Colima Ranch
Willacy

Schaleben Interests
Hidalgo

Tecomate Ranch Properties
Dr. Byron Brown
Dr. Steve Byrd
Dr. Gary M. Schwarz
Dr. Frank Shepard
Dr. Steve Shepard
Dr. Tom Spicer
Dr. Fred Voorhees
Starr

Jack Scoggins Jr.
Starr Feedyards, Inc.
Starr

Larry and Betty Lou Sherrin
La Brisa Ranch Partnership
Starr

Charles Shofner
Diamond S Ranch
Willacy

Ana, Jaime and Leticia Tijerina
Caramacaro Ranch
Willacy

Rick and Irma Tijerina
Tierra Colorada Ranch
Starr

Benito and Toni Treviño
Rancho Lomitas Native Plant Nursery
Starr

Harold and Maxine Turk
La Escondida Ranch
Hidalgo

Baldo Jr. and Daniel Vela
San Pedro Ranch
Hidalgo

Robert and Isabel Vezzetti
Vezzetti Ranch
Willacy

Romeo Villarreal
Jesus Maria Ranch
Hidalgo

Tony and Sharon Vindell
Cameron

Leticia M. Volpe
Varal Ranches LTD
Zapata

Sharon Waite and Joe Metz
Waite-Metz Farms
Hidalgo

Thomas H. Watkins
La Hacienda de Las Retamas
Cameron

Wayne and Chris Westphal
Palm Gardens, Inc.
Hidalgo

Winifred Wetegrove
Las Majadas Ranch
Willacy

L. Nathan Winters
Winters' Ranch
Hidalgo

Fausto Yturria
Hacienda Yturria
Kenedy

Frank D. Yturria
Yturria Ranch
Willacy

Roberto and Fran Yzaguirre
Starr

PHOTO BOOK PATRONS

250 or more
Knapp Medical Center
Rio Grande Regional Hospital
Valley Baptist Health System

100 or more
Charles Clark Chevrolet Co.
Loring Cook Foundation
The Nature Conservancy of Texas

50 or more
A.G. Edwards & Sons, Inc.
    Corpus Christi – Roger Zessin
Clark-Knapp Honda of McAllen
Hollon Oil Company
Inn at Chachalaca Bend
McAllen Chamber of Commerce
McAllen National Bank
Shepard Walton King Insurance Group
Sierra Title
Texas State Bank
Tipotex Chevrolet
University of Texas Pan American Foundation

20 or more
A.G. Edwards & Sons, Inc.
    Brownsville – Hal Morrow
    Corpus Christi – Matt P. Paul
    McAllen – Dennis Burleson
    McAllen – Greg Douglas
    McAllen – Bill Martin
    McAllen – Pat A. McClellan
Advertir
Alamo Bank of Texas
Allen Floral by Betty

The Appraisal Company
Steve Bentsen and Laura Moore
Bentsen Palm Development
Mr. and Mrs. Bob Boggus
Boultinghouse Simpson Architects
Carol Rausch Braden
Britton's Photo & Imaging
Bill Burns
Cantu Lease, Inc.
Carter & Associates
Castellano Ranch
Chevy Suburban
Children's Dental Center – Phil and Karen Hunke
Kirk, Jeri, Alex and Daniel Clark
Closner Equipment Co., Inc.
Coastal Banc – Rio Grande Valley
Steven and Lisa Cofoid
Country Casuals
Rip and Laurie Davenport
Val and Vern Denman
Descon Construction, L.P. –
    Mickey C. Smith and Wayne Medlin
Edinburg Chamber of Commerce
Edinburg Improvement Association
El Clavo Lumber Co., Inc.
Ellis, Koeneke & Ramirez, LLP
Randall and Carolyn Ennis
Enterprise Rent-A-Car
Delmar W. and Dora Valverde Fankhauser
First National Bank
First National Bank of San Benito
Sean Fitzgerald and Jeremy Woodhouse
Foremost Paving

Frank Smith Toyota
Friends of the Wildlife Corridor
Frost Bank
G & S Asphalt Sealers / Pavers
Sue Ann and J.A. Garcia Jr.
David and Diane Garza –
    El Monte del Rancho Viejo
Tony Garza, Texas Railroad Commissioner
General Motors Acceptance Corporation
Glick Twins
Matt and Patty Gorges
Greater Mission Chamber of Commerce
Arturo and Barbara Guerra
Guerra Brothers Successors
H. Yturria Land & Cattle Co.
Harlingen Area Chamber of Commerce
Glenn Hayes and Bill Draker
Carla C. and Kenneth M. Haynes
Rex Hewitt
Dr. Stephen and Colleen Hook
Mr. and Mrs. Larry T. Hunter
Charles Hury and Dr. Oscar Sotelo
IMS Health Care, Inc. –
    Bill Carlson and Linda Gardner
Inter National Bank
International Bank of Commerce
Glenn and Pat Jarvis
Johnson Brothers Construction
Jones & Cook Stationers
JP Morgan Chase
JS Media
Neal and Wileen King
Kittleman, Thomas, Ramirez & Gonzales

PHOTO BOOK PATRONS

Kolder
Kreidler Funeral Home, Inc.
KRGV Eyewitness News
Greg Lasley and Larry Ditto
Marion R. Lawler Jr. M.D.
Lifetime Industries, Inc.
Lifetime Investments
Dr. and Mrs. Ford Lockett
Lone Star National Bank
Long, Chilton, LLP
Lynne Tate Real Estate
Magic Valley Electric Cooperative
Martin Farm and Ranch
John and Audrey Martin
Georgia and Sam Mason
Millicent and Howard I. Mason Jr.
City of McAllen
Margaret and Robert McAllen
McAllen International Museum
McAllen-Miller International Airport
McAllen North Rotary Club
Ben and Linda McCampbell
John and Judy McClung
John B. McFarland
Midway Companies
Charles F. Mild, M.D.
The Monitor
Ann Maddox Moore
Pete and Vicki Moore
MO-VAC Service Co., Inc.
Patricia Moyer
Naturally Curious, Inc., at Alamo Inn
Nuevo Santander Gallery

Passmore, Walker & Twenhafel, LLP
Payne Auto Group
Buck and Penny Pettitt
Professional Appraisal Services, Inc.
Quips 'N' Quotes
Rio Bank
Luis and Mary Ann Rios
Bill and Susie Robertson
Ron Smith Bird Carvings
Donna, Jim and David Rowland
Russell Plantation
Sabal Palm Audubon Center and Sanctuary
St. John's Episcopal Day School
San Pedro Ranch
Schaleben Limited Partnership
Service Group
Dr. Frank E. Shepard
Dr. Stephen P. Shepard
Wayne and Reba Showers
Smith-Reagan Insurance Agency
Speer Ranch
Spikes Ford
Larry and Ellen Stone
Sun Valley Motor Hotel
Sweet Temptations
Dr. Janet L. Tate and Hugh E. Hackney
Molly Thornberry
Tipton Motors, Inc.
George and June Toland
University of Texas Pan American
Tom Urban
Valley Advertising Federation
Valley Beverage − Miller / Coors

Valley Chevy Dealers
  Bert Ogden Chevrolet
  Charles Clark Chevrolet
  Kellogg Chevrolet
  Knapp Chevrolet
  Payne Weslaco Motors
  Rio Motor Company
  Roberts Chevrolet
  Tipotex Chevrolet
Valley Design
Valley Morning Star
Valley Mortgage Company, Inc.
Valley Nature Center
Van Burkleo Motors, Inc.
Betty and Roscoe Watkins
Sheldon and Eve Weisfeld
Wells Fargo
Wild Bird Center − Harlingen
Willamar Gin Co., Inc.
Mr. and Mrs. Henry Willms −
  Willms Engineering & Surveying
Mary A. and Frank D. Yturria
Roberto and Fran Yzaguirre

Book Patron Committee

Kirk A. Clark, Chairman	Wes Kittleman
Alice G.K.K. East	John Martin
Colleen Hook	Sam Mason
Ruth Hoyt	Judy McClung
Karen Hunke	Bill Robertson
Neal King Jr.	Wayne Showers

PHOTO BOOK CONTRIBUTORS

Managing Editor .... *Ron Smith*
Copy Editor .... *Jan Epton Seale*
Advisors .... *Colleen Hook*
Ruth Hoyt
John Martin
Sam Mason

Contributing Authors
Preface .... *Ron Smith*
The Legacy of Conservation .... *Kirk Clark*
VLF Wildlife Photo Contest IV .... *John and Gloria Tveten*
VLF Wildlife Photographers of the Year .... *Larry Ditto and Greg Lasley*
The VLF Landowners of the Year .... *Bud and Jimmy Payne*
Second Grand Prize-winning Photographers .... *Bill Draker and Glenn Hayes*
Second Grand Prize-winning Landowners .... *Gary Schwarz, Steve Shepard and Partners - Tecomate Ranch*
Third Grand Prize-winning Photographers .... *Sean Fitzgerald and Jeremy Woodhouse*
Third Grand Prize-winning Landowners .... *Roberto and Fran Yzaguirre*
Fourth Grand Prize-winning Photographers .... *Derrick Hamrick and Roberta E. Summers*
Fourth Grand Prize-winning Landowners .... *Jim and Kathy Collins and Carolyn Cook Landrum - Cook Ranch Properties*
Fifth Grand Prize-winning Photographer .... *Tom Urban*
Fifth Grand Prize-winning Landowners .... *King Ranch*
Birds Essay .... *Father Tom Pincelli*
Mammals Essay .... *Stephen Labuda*
Insects and Arachnids Essay .... *Carrie Cate*
Reptiles and Amphibians Essay .... *Colette Adams*
Special Categories Essay .... *Joanna Rivera*
Photo Contest Judges .... *Steve Freligh, Darrell Gulin, Wyman Meinzer*
The Fourth Grade Nature Photo Contest .... *Richard Moore*
The Valley Land Fund Story .... *John and Audrey Martin*
Afterword .... *Ron Smith*
Consultants .... *Colette Adams*
Benton Basham
Ray Bieber and Lynn Bieber-Weir
Carrie Cate
Larry Ditto
Billie Hoffmann
Greg Lasley
Father Tom Pincelli
John and Gloria Tveten
2000 Photo Contest Coordinator .... *Lisa Hettler*
Typist .... *Laura Martin*
Printing Coordination and Color Work .... *Bob Carter, Carter and Associates*
Design .... *Don Breeden and Robert J. Scott, Breeden/McCumber/Gonzalez*
Printer .... *Lin Miller – Gateway Printing*
Published by .... *Valley Land Fund, Inc.*

THE VALLEY LAND FUND STORY

"It was so much fun and so rewarding," said John Martin, recalling how a core group of conservationists purchased 2¼ acres of pristine native brush south of Weslaco that was destined to be bulldozed.

Visiting after a Frontera Audubon Society meeting one night in the fall of 1986, Steve Bentsen, Clayton and Lynette Scribner and John and Audrey Martin decided to offer the owner of the valuable land $10,000 for half of it, suggesting he donate the other half so that the entire acreage could be preserved for its abundant wildlife.

Before the year was out, the deal was closed. Thus began The Valley Land Fund, a group organized to encourage the preservation of habitat for wildlife in the Lower Rio Grande Valley of Texas. "We knew we were on the right track," John Martin said.

July 1987 saw the first organizational meeting of the founding members, who were John Martin, Tom Koeneke, Carol Rausch Braden, Jack Hart, Steve Bentsen and Audrey Martin. By October, by-laws were approved and they had been joined by other founding board members: Joe Charles Ballenger, Don Farst, Mark Feldman, Juliet Garcia, Kevin Hiles, Bill Hollon, Henry Kawahata, Jim McAllen, T. Edward Mercer, William Peck, Gayle Runnels, Martha Russell, Gary Schwarz, Mike Thatcher and Frank Yturria.

"From the beginning, we determined that our

Jim Goin/Neal and Gayle Runnels

group would not promote controversy or be political in our methods. We would say nothing about lands that had already been cleared. We would simply work to preserve what precious little was left," John Martin explained. The group would focus on a common interest that excluded no interested parties.

Audrey Martin observed, "We wanted to concentrate on those pieces that were not in the purview of state or federal programs, land that would otherwise be lost forever. As it happened, we have been most successful acting as catalyst and intermediary, helping to secure lands for both programs and other organizations and agencies." At that time, less than three percent of original Valley habitat remained. After thirteen years of explosive growth, that percent has undoubtedly diminished.

From 1987 to 1996, the board met twice a year to set major policy and review activities, leaving day-to-day activities to the six-member founding executive committee. John and Audrey Martin shouldered the major load of work, with John as president and Audrey as an executive board advisor.

Karen Hunke succeeded John as president in 1996. With Karen's guidance in organization and procedures, the board expanded and members became increasingly pro-active. Since that time, the board meets six times a year, with executive board meetings monthly, and many committees at work weekly on specific assignments.

In 1994, The Valley Land Fund launched its biannual Wildlife Photo Contest. The photographic images of the fourth such contest rest within the covers of the book you hold. Colleen Curran Hook, as photo contest coordinator, worked tirelessly through the 1996 contest, becoming director of programs in 1998. Lisa Hettler became contest coordinator for 2000.

Succeeding to the presidency in 1998 was Wes Kittleman. His work stabilized the group during a period of expansion and brought great improvement in legal and fiscal procedures.

In January 2001, Neal King Jr. took the president's gavel. Neal brings to the post a great love for and extensive knowledge about the South Texas brush country, and fervor to educate our young people to the wonders of their surroundings.

The work of The Valley Land Fund has grown greatly over the years as goals and needs have been identified. Besides the 42-member volunteer board, the Fund utilizes four paid employees: Colleen Hook, director of programs; Laura Miller, membership and education coordinator; Ruth Hoyt, photo contest director; and Sam Mason, assistant

John and Gloria Tveten/Rosemary and Cleve Breedlove

photo contest director. And several hundred Friends of The Valley Land Fund are doing their part by joining with a modest annual membership fee, supporting the Fund's efforts in fundraising, and helping educate others about our unique land.

The Valley Land Fund offices are located at 2400 North 10th Street, Suite A, in McAllen, Texas.

John and Audrey Martin
Edinburg, Texas

John and Audrey Martin are founders and board members of The Valley Land Fund. The Wildlife Photo Contest was John's idea as a way of adding economics to conservation. He and Audrey have dedicated the past seven years to the success of this ever-expanding endeavor.

The Valley Land Fund

is dedicated to preserving the remaining three to five percent of the natural habitat of the Lower Rio Grande Valley of Texas and to protecting the native plants and wildlife as a heritage for future generations.

Today, the VLF is working to preserve natural habitats and wildlife through the protection of land by purchase or gift and by rewarding the private landowner for responsible stewardship. In addition, the VLF is dedicated to educating people to be environmentally aware and responsible. Programs include the Wildlife Photo Contest, the Fourth Grade Nature Photo Contest, exhibitions, educational materials and color photo books such as this one.

Previous Books:
Treasures of South Texas (1995)
Creatures on the Edge (1997)
The Lens and the Land (1999)

Fourth Grade Nature Photo Contest

Nicholas Norris, St. John's Episcopal School

AFTERWORD

First Hawk Over the Valley

The Broadwing aloft
in late morning on warm air rising.
A long Skyride from his Southland wintering.
His dark eyes mirror
a bright arcing waterway below.
His keen eyes see
hard boxes and paths where humans live,
spread across the level, heated plain
to the horizon.
Yet along the cloud-reflecting water,
green banks offer safety, food and rest.

He folds his wide wings . . . they spill air.
He drops . . . he drifts . . . his head swinging,
searching along the river.
Skimming treetops, swiftly he slants into shelter.
A great Cedar Elm where he perches, hidden,
awake to the movements in the thorny undergrowth
below his flexing talons.

Rio Bravo . . . Rio del Norte . . . Rio Grande.
To him, respite from a journey halfway only
to his Northland summering.
He is the First of thousands.
Each year for millennia
there has always been a First Hawk.

How many more will stop here?
And for how many more years
will there be places for them?

And for us?

Ron Smith

Sean Fitzgerald and Jeremy Woodhouse/ Roberto and Fran Yzaguirre

More than 99% of all species that have ever lived on earth are extinct.